Sunset
Cooking
for Two

**By the Editors of Sunset Books
and Sunset Magazine**

Lane Publishing Co. • Menlo Park, California

Great Recipes Tailored to Size

Whatever your reason for dining à *deux*, here's a book full of special dishes cut down to size for you and your companion.

Everything is easier when you are two . . . grocery shopping, food preparation, cleanup. With only two schedules to be considered, your eating hours can be as flexible as you both like; so can the place you choose to dine, for it's not much of a balancing trick to carry two plates to the fireside, TV room, or patio.

With this book, you can tell at a glance how much time each recipe will take. A little clock symbol ⏲ identifies this information, which appears under each recipe title.

We've tailored our soup, salad, sandwich, and egg/cheese chapters for the working couple all too familiar with the effect that business lunches can have on dinner appetites. The meat, poultry, and seafood chapters offer heartier entrées still with no leftovers to deal with. Recipes especially suited for cooking in a microwave oven are featured in their own section.

For-one cooks will also find the book useful, since a number of recipes appear in for-one quantities, while virtually all the others—even if made in for-two proportions—will yield leftovers to please, not to inundate. Each recipe makes two servings unless otherwise indicated.

We wish to extend thanks to Diane L. Dyson and Rebecca La Brum for their special assistance in the preparation of this book.

Supervising Editor: **Judith A. Gaulke**

Research & Text: **Cynthia Scheer**
Elaine Woodard

Special Consultant: **Joan Griffiths**

Design: **Cynthia Hanson**

Illustrations: **Mary Knowles**
Sandra Popovich

Photography: **Nikolay Zurek** 18, 26, 31, 34, 39, 42, 47, 51, 54, 59, 62, 67, 70, 75.

Kathryn Kleinman 23, 78.

Photo Editor: **Lynne B. Morrall**

Cover: Quick, hearty, and colorful, Chicken Primavera (page 53) makes an elegant dinner for two. Golden chicken breasts are cloaked with a creamy, vegetable-laden sauce, then nestled atop beds of cooked pasta. Photograph by Kathryn Kleinman. Design by Lynne B. Morrall.

Editor, Sunset Books: Elizabeth L. Hogan

Fourth printing May 1989

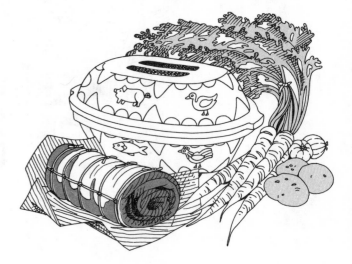

CONTENTS

SOUPS

Great soup once meant enormous pots of fragrant ingredients that required hours of simmering and resulted in days of leftovers for all but the largest of families. Then there was okay soup, the kind you got by opening a can and adding some milk or water.

This chapter brings you the best of both—recipes for soups that are great, in quantities just right for two (or for one, with one handy serving left to enjoy another day), and with much of the convenience and speed of canned soups. Indeed, many start with canned broth and go on to such special touches as vegetables that still have crunch, bits of crisp bacon, chunks of tender seafood or spicy sausage, spinach-laden meatballs, dollops of cool sour cream. Some can be made ahead, served chilled or reheated to be enjoyed later.

Soup is perfectly portable —when you're in a mood to sit by the fire or on the patio and exchange events of the day, or to relax and let TV bring you up to date on events in the world, a mug of steaming soup is convenient and satisfying.

These recipes begin with light soups, the kind that round out a sandwich or salad meal. Next come the hearty soups that are a meal on their own, well able to satisfy the most enthusiastic appetite with nothing more than some good bread alongside.

Creamy Mushroom Soup

Preparation time (cooking included): 10 minutes

A rich-tasting soup without the calories, this one whips up in minutes. Sip it from a mug, accompanied by a salad or sandwich.

- 1½ tablespoons butter or margarine
- ¼ pound mushrooms, coarsely chopped
- 1 small onion, coarsely chopped
- 1 tablespoon all-purpose flour
- 2 cups milk
- 1 chicken bouillon cube
- ⅛ teaspoon thyme leaves
  Salt and pepper

In a wide frying pan, melt butter over medium heat. Add mushrooms and onion; cook, stirring, until onion is limp and juices evaporate. Stir in flour and cook until bubbly; remove from heat. Gradually stir in milk. Add bouillon cube (breaking up with spoon) and thyme leaves. Cook, stirring constantly, until thickened.

Whirl soup in a blender or food processor until smooth. Add salt and pepper to taste.

Curried Broccoli Soup

Preparation time (cooking included): 10 minutes

Cool, green broccoli purée comes alive with a nip of curry. Garnish servings with chopped salted peanuts. It's good hot or cold. (See photograph on page 34.)

- 1½ tablespoons butter or margarine
- 1 small onion, chopped
- ¾ teaspoon curry powder
- 1 can (about 14 oz.) regular-strength chicken broth
- 1 package (10 oz.) frozen chopped broccoli, thawed
  Sour cream
  Chopped salted peanuts

In a 3-quart pan, melt butter over medium heat; add onion and curry powder and cook until onion is limp. Stir in broth and broccoli and cook, covered, until broccoli is heated through and fork tender (about 3 minutes).

Whirl soup, a portion at a time, in a blender or food processor until smooth. Serve hot or cold; reheat if made ahead. Top with a dollop of sour cream and a sprinkling of chopped peanuts.

Quick Gazpacho

Ⓢ *Preparation time: 10 minutes. Chilling time: 30 minutes*

Served icy cold, this chunky gazpacho is quick to put together and can be made a day ahead. (See photograph on page 18.)

- ⅓ **cup chopped cucumber**
- ¼ **cup finely chopped mild red or white onion**
- 1 **small avocado, peeled, pitted, and diced**
- ¼ **teaspoon oregano leaves, crumbled**
- 1½ **tablespoons olive oil or salad oil**
- 1 **tablespoon wine vinegar**
- 2 **cups tomato juice**
   Salt and pepper
   Ice cubes (optional)
   Lime wedges

In a serving bowl or pitcher, combine cucumber, onion, avocado, oregano, oil, and vinegar. Pour in tomato juice. Cover and chill thoroughly. Add salt and pepper to taste. Add ice cubes to individual servings, if you wish. Pass lime wedges to squeeze over.

Pacific Halibut Soup

Ⓢ *Preparation time: 10 minutes. Cooking time: 30 minutes*

You add the fish to this soup at the very last minute, and it stays moist and flaky in the seasoned tomato broth with rice and green beans. With warm garlic-buttered French bread, it makes a perfect supper.

- 1 **tablespoon olive oil or salad oil**
- 1 **medium-size onion, chopped**
- 1 **small clove garlic, minced or pressed**
- ⅓ **cup thinly sliced celery**
- 1 **can (1 lb.) tomatoes**
- 1 **can (about 14 oz.) regular-strength chicken broth**
- ½ **teaspoon Italian herb seasoning or ¼ teaspoon *each* oregano leaves and dry basil**
- 2 **tablespoons rice**
- 1 **cup frozen cut green beans, thawed**
- ½ **to ¾ pound halibut, thawed if frozen**
   Salt and pepper
   Chopped parsley
   Grated Parmesan cheese (optional)

Heat oil in a heavy 4-quart pan over medium heat; add onion, garlic, and celery. Cook, stirring, until onion is limp. Stir in tomatoes (break up with a spoon) and their liquid, broth, Italian herbs, and rice. Cover and simmer for 15 minutes. Add beans and simmer, covered, for about 10 minutes longer or until rice and beans are tender to bite.

Meanwhile, remove skin and bones from fish and cut into about 1-inch pieces. Add to soup and simmer just until fish flakes readily when prodded with a fork (about 5 minutes). Season with salt and pepper to taste. Sprinkle individual servings with parsley and pass Parmesan cheese to spoon over each serving, if you wish.

Sherry Clam Chowder

Ⓢ *Preparation time (cooking included): 15 minutes*

Sprinkle crisp bacon over chowder at the last minute and garnish with spoonfuls of sour cream.

- 4 **slices bacon, cut in small pieces**
- 1 **medium-size onion, finely chopped**
- ½ **cup finely chopped celery**
- 1 **can (about 11 oz.) condensed cream of potato soup**
- 1 **bottle (8 oz.) clam juice**
- ½ **cup milk or half-and-half (light cream)**
- 1 **can (7 oz.) minced clams**
- 1 **tablespoon dry sherry**
   Salt and pepper
   Sour cream

In a 3-quart pan over medium heat, cook bacon until crisp; set aside. Discard all but 2 tablespoons of the drippings. Add onion and celery and cook until limp, stirring occasionally. Add potato soup, clam juice, milk, and minced clams and their liquid; heat through, stirring. Stir in sherry, add salt and pepper to taste, and sprinkle over reserved bacon. Top with spoonfuls of sour cream.

Lazy Cioppino

⏱ Preparation time (cooking included): 10 minutes

No cracking of shells or cleaning of shrimp here. Just buy crab and shrimp meat at the fish market, open a few cans, heat, and you have cioppino!

- **2 tablespoons butter or olive oil**
- **1 small onion, finely chopped**
- **1 clove garlic, minced or pressed**
- **¼ teaspoon *each* oregano leaves and crumbled bay leaves**
  Dash sage
- **1 can (14 oz.) pear-shaped tomatoes**
- **1 tablespoon tomato-based chili sauce**
- **1 can (8 oz.) tomato sauce**
- **¼ pound *each* crab meat and small cooked shrimp**
  Water (optional)
  Salt and pepper

Melt butter in a 2-quart pan and cook onion and garlic over medium heat until limp. Stir in oregano, bay, sage, tomatoes (break up with a spoon) and their liquid, chili sauce, tomato sauce, crab, and shrimp; heat through. Add water for thinner soup, if you wish, and salt and pepper to taste.

Cabbage and Ham Soup

⏱ Preparation time (cooking included): 15 minutes

Chunks of ham, purchased from a deli or left over from baked ham, are added to sautéed cabbage in a light broth. Top with dollops of sour cream.

- **3 tablespoons butter or margarine**
- **2 tablespoons finely chopped celery**
- **¼ cup finely chopped onion**
- **1 tablespoon chopped parsley**
- **1 tablespoon all-purpose flour**
- **1 can (about 14 oz.) regular-strength chicken broth**
- **½ pound cooked ham, diced**
- **½ teaspoon crumbled bay leaf**
- **1 cup finely shredded cabbage**
  Sour cream

Melt 2 tablespoons of the butter in a 2-quart pan over medium heat; add celery, onion, and parsley and cook until limp. Stir in flour. Add broth and cook, stirring, until bubbly. Add ham, bay leaf, cabbage, and remaining 1 tablespoon butter; cook until ham is heated through and cabbage is limp.

Spoon sour cream into individual portions.

Vegetable-Cheese Soup

⏱ Preparation time: 15 minutes. Cooking time: 15 minutes

Instant mashed potatoes and canned chicken broth speed the making of this vegetable soup. Stir in cheese chunks just before serving.

- **2 tablespoons butter or margarine**
- **1 medium-size onion, minced**
- **2 large carrots, cut into thin diagonal slices**
- **1 stalk celery, cut into thin diagonal slices**
- **1 can (about 14 oz.) regular-strength chicken broth**
  Instant mashed potatoes (amount for 2 servings), prepared according to package directions
- **½ cup milk**
- **¼ teaspoon *each* seasoned salt and celery seed**
  Dash pepper
  About 3 ounces jack or Cheddar cheese, diced
  Ground mace (optional)

Melt butter in a 3-quart pan over medium heat; add onion and cook until limp. Add carrots, celery, and chicken broth. Cover and cook over low heat until vegetables are fork tender (about 10 minutes). Remove from heat and stir in prepared instant mashed potatoes. Add milk, seasoned salt, celery seed, and pepper.

Return to heat until hot through—do not boil. Remove from heat, add cheese, cover pan, and let stand 5 minutes until cheese partially melts. Sprinkle lightly with mace, if you wish.

Eggplant Supper Soup

⏱ *Preparation time: 10 minutes. Cooking time: 40 minutes*

Another full-meal soup, starring ground beef, can be made in less than an hour and you can ignore it for about half of that time.

- 1 tablespoon olive oil or salad oil
- 1 tablespoon butter or margarine
- 1 small onion, chopped
- ½ pound lean ground beef
- 1 small eggplant (about 1 lb.), diced
- 1 small clove garlic, minced or pressed
- 1 small carrot, shredded
- 1 can (14 oz.) pear-shaped tomatoes
- 1 can (about 14 oz.) regular-strength beef broth
- ½ teaspoon *each* salt and sugar
- ¼ teaspoon *each* pepper and ground nutmeg
- 2 tablespoons *each* salad macaroni and minced parsley
  Grated Parmesan cheese

Heat oil and butter in a 3-quart pan over medium heat; add onion and cook, stirring, until limp. Crumble meat into pan and stir over medium-high heat until it loses its pinkness. Skim off and discard fat. Add eggplant, garlic, carrot, tomatoes (breaking them up with a spoon) and their liquid, beef broth, salt, sugar, pepper, and nutmeg. Cover and simmer for about 30 minutes.

Add macaroni and parsley and simmer for 10 to 15 minutes more or until macaroni is tender to bite. Pass cheese to sprinkle over servings.

Portuguese Sausage Soup

⏱ *Preparation time: 10 minutes. Cooking time: 30 minutes*

Potatoes, spinach, and sausage make this a sturdy soup, worthy of top billing for a cold-weather supper. Hot cornbread would go well with it; so would a salad of shredded carrots.

- 2 medium-size potatoes, peeled and thinly sliced (about 1 lb.)
- 1 medium-size onion, thinly sliced
- 1 can (about 14 oz.) regular-strength chicken broth
- ½ cup water
- ⅛ teaspoon pepper
- ¾ pound spinach
- ½ pound linguisa or chorizo sausage
  Boiling water
- 1 tablespoon butter or margarine

In a 3-quart pan, combine potatoes, onion, broth, the ½ cup water, and pepper; bring to a boil, reduce heat, cover, and simmer until vegetables are fork tender (about 25 minutes).

Meanwhile, remove and discard spinach stems; rinse leaves well, drain, and cut into very fine, short shreds. Set aside. Place sausage in a frying pan with about ½ inch boiling water; simmer, covered, for 15 minutes. Drain, remove casing, and cut into thin slanting slices or crumble; set aside.

Whirl potato mixture in a blender or food processor until smooth; return puréed mixture to pan. Add butter and spinach and cook over low heat, uncovered, for about 3 minutes or until greens are wilted but still bright green. Stir in reserved sausage and heat through.

Spinach Meatball Minestrone

⏱ *Preparation time: 20 minutes. Cooking time: 25 minutes*

A good choice for a busy day, spinach meatball minestrone tastes as if it takes hours to make.

  Spinach meatballs (recipe follows)
  Butter or margarine
- 1 can (14 oz.) regular-strength beef broth
- 1 can (8 oz.) stewed tomatoes
- 1 can (8 oz.) kidney beans
- ¼ teaspoon *each* oregano leaves and dry basil
- ¼ cup *each* sliced carrot and celery
- ¼ cup elbow or bow-shaped macaroni
  Parmesan cheese

(Continued on next page)

In a wide frying pan, brown meatballs in butter, if needed, over medium heat; remove from pan as browned.

In a 3-quart pan, pour beef broth, tomatoes (breaking up with a spoon) and their liquid, beans and their liquid, oregano, basil, carrot, celery, and meatballs. Cover and bring to a boil. Reduce heat and cook over medium heat for 15 minutes or until vegetables are tender and meatballs cooked through; skim off any accumulated fat.

Stir in macaroni, cover, and cook until tender to bite (about 10 minutes). Sprinkle servings with Parmesan cheese.

Spinach meatballs. Squeeze liquid from 1 package (10 oz.) **frozen chopped spinach,** thawed; mix with ½ pound **lean ground beef,** 2 tablespoons **fine dry bread crumbs,** 1 **egg,** ¼ teaspoon **salt,** dash **pepper,** and 1 small **onion,** finely chopped. Shape into 1-inch balls.

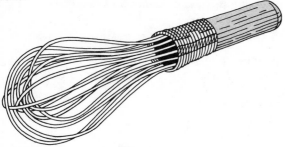

Greek Meatball Soup

 Preparation time: 15 minutes. Cooking time: 30 minutes

Tiny meatballs simmer in the stock of this hearty supper soup, which cooks in less than 45 minutes. With it, nibble crisp Armenian cracker bread or bread sticks.

- 1 **tablespoon butter or margarine**
- 1 **medium-size onion, finely chopped**
- 2 **cans (14 oz. *each*) regular-strength beef broth**
- ½ **pound lean ground beef**
- 1 **tablespoon rice**
- 1 **small clove garlic, minced or pressed**
- ¼ **teaspoon salt**
- ⅛ **teaspoon oregano leaves, crumbled**
- ⅓ **cup finely chopped parsley**
- 1 **tablespoon cornstarch blended with 2 tablespoons cold water**
- ⅓ **cup *each* whipping cream and shredded Parmesan cheese**
- **Chopped green onions**
- **Shredded Parmesan cheese**

Melt butter in a 3-quart pan. Add onion and cook, stirring, over medium heat until limp. Remove ⅓ of

the onion from pan and set aside. Add beef broth to pan; cover and simmer while shaping meatballs.

Mix together ground beef, reserved sautéed onion, rice, garlic, salt, and oregano; shape into marble-size balls. Roll in parsley and drop into bubbling broth. Cover and simmer for 25 minutes.

Stir cornstarch mixture into simmering soup. Mix together cream and the ⅓ cup Parmesan; ladle about ½ cup hot broth into cheese mixture, stirring constantly; then return to pan, stirring. Cook and stir a few minutes longer until soup boils and thickens slightly. Pass small bowls of green onion and Parmesan cheese to spoon over.

Maritata Soup

 Preparation time (cooking included): 15 minutes

Use either canned broth or your own homemade broth to make this Italian soup. When you serve it as a light main dish, add crusty bread, a salad such as Belgian endive with a tart dressing, and a fruit dessert.

- 4 **cups regular-strength beef or chicken broth**
- 1 **to 2 ounces vermicelli**
- ¼ **cup unsalted butter, at room temperature**
- ⅓ **cup freshly grated Parmesan cheese**
- 2 **egg yolks**
- ½ **cup whipping cream**

Bring broth to a boil in a 2 to 3-quart pan. Add vermicelli (broken into shorter lengths, if you wish) and boil, uncovered, for 7 to 9 minutes or until tender to bite. Meanwhile, in a bowl blend butter with cheese and egg yolks, then gradually beat in cream. Spoon a little hot broth into cream mixture, stirring constantly; then return to pan and cook, stirring constantly, until heated through.

Chopstick Soups

Some very satisfying whole-meal soups can start with an easy-to-fix Oriental noodle soup mix. The package contains precooked noodles that take only 2 or 3 minutes to prepare, a packet of soup base for the broth, and sometimes other seasonings. Look for packages among the Oriental foods in your market.

You can also buy Oriental-style noodles alone—combine them with canned broth and some interesting ingredients of your own (several suggestions follow), and you'll probably find that your creations are the best of all.

Understanding the labels

Before you shop, make at least a mental note of these four definitions; they'll help you understand the often confusing package labels.

The word *mein* (pronounced *meen*, incidentally) is a general Chinese name for noodles. The Japanese word *somem* means thin, round noodles, and *udon* is the word for wide, flat ones. *Saimin* is Hawaii's version of noodle soup.

Because most Oriental noodles contain no egg—and U. S. Government regulations require that egg be an ingredient in a product labeled noodles—the Oriental products are often called alimentary paste or imitation noodles.

Most soup mixes have cooking directions in English; on those that don't, you'll often find guidance in the form of little drawings. Each package makes at least one generous serving, but it will serve two people if you add bits of cooked meats, eggs, fish, or vegetables.

It's fun to serve the soup with chopsticks (for eating the noodles, meat, and vegetables) and an Oriental or regular soup spoon for the broth.

Making the noodle part...

With or without a mix, it's only a matter of minutes from empty pan to fragrant, noodle-filled, bubbling broth.

To make noodle soup from a mix, follow directions on the package. If the directions aren't readable, do this: Bring 2 to 3 cups salted water to a boil, add noodles, and boil until tender (usually 2 or 3 minutes). Add soup base and about 1 cup of any cooked meats and vegetables you choose; stir and heat through. Remove from heat and serve in large soup bowls, arranging some of the colorful added ingredients attractively on top. Sprinkle with sliced green onion, minced parsley, or chopped fresh coriander (cilantro), if you wish.

To make noodle soup from scratch, cook 2 to 3 ounces Oriental noodles, regular noodles, or vermicelli in 2 to 3 cups boiling salted water until just tender to bite (start testing in about 2 minutes, as some cook quickly); drain. Heat 1 can (about 14 oz.) regular-strength chicken broth or beef broth to boiling, add drained noodles, 1 teaspoon soy sauce, and about 1 cup meat or vegetables of your choice (suggestions follow). Heat through and serve as directed above.

...and adding the zest

Think in terms of combinations of the following ingredients (all cut into bite-size pieces), and the possibilities for adding flavor and texture become almost infinite.

Cooked meats, such as beef, pork, ham, or lamb; Chinese barbecued pork (called *chahr siu*, available in Oriental stores); chicken, turkey, or duck.

Fish and shellfish, such as cooked or canned fish, shrimp, crab, clams, or abalone; Japanese steamed fish cake (called *kamaboko*), sliced.

Eggs, hard-cooked, sliced, and arranged on top of soup just before serving. Or drop a raw egg (or just the yolk) into center of bowl of hot soup and swirl through for flavor.

Vegetables, such as cooked carrots, green beans, celery, mushrooms, soaked dried mushrooms. Or add raw spinach leaves, Chinese cabbage, Chinese edible pod peas, or bean sprouts to the boiling water and cook briefly along with the noodles.

SALADS

"Let's just have a salad tonight." This is a frequent rallying cry among people accustomed to business lunches, concerned about diet, living with irregular dinner hours, too busy to stop and "cook" dinner.

It's a boon to be able to grab ingredients from the cupboard or refrigerator and combine them with fresh lettuce or other salad greens or fresh fruit for a quick and wonderful meal. One trick is to keep cans of tuna, salmon, crab, ham, and shrimp on hand. Another is to have sliced meats from the deli in your freezer to pull out for last-minute use. An assortment of cheeses will also be useful, along with citrus fruits and raisins—these foods take to relatively long storage and do great things for salads.

The recipes in this chapter offer a taste of Mexico, the Orient, and Vietnam, as well as more typically American pairing of such ingredients as ham and turkey, chicken and fruit.

Few foods have more visual appeal or more variations than salads. They can be the focal point of any meal, hearty enough to stand on their own; they can share the spotlight with soup and crusty French bread; or they can be simply the crisp, fresh prelude, postlude, or accompaniment to a meal that features a more elaborate entrée.

Ham and Turkey Salad

Preparation time (cooking included): 20 minutes.
Chilling time: 15 minutes

A curry-flavored dressing distinguishes this attractive salad. Complement it with hot corn muffins.

- ½ cup slivered almonds
- 1½ cups diced cooked turkey
- ½ cup diced cooked ham (or cut in matchstick-size pieces)
- 1 small red-skinned apple
- 2 teaspoons lemon juice
- ½ cup *each* seedless grapes and mayonnaise
- ¾ teaspoon soy sauce
- ½ teaspoon curry powder
  Crisp salad greens
  Small grape clusters (optional)

Spread almonds in a shallow pan and toast in a 350° oven for 8 to 10 minutes or until golden; set aside.

Combine turkey, ham, and ⅓ cup of the toasted almonds. Core and thinly slice apple and coat with lemon juice; add to meat. Stir in the ½ cup grapes. Blend mayonnaise with soy and curry; pour over salad. Press into a 4 to 5-cup bowl, cover, and chill at least 15 minutes. Turn out on a bed of greens. Garnish with remaining toasted almonds and surround with grape clusters, if you wish.

Mexican Mixed Salad

Preparation time: 15 minutes

Chef's salad, Mexican-style, combines julienne strips of meat or chicken with typical flavors from south of the border—chili, coriander, lime. You serve it with avocado and orange slices on a bed of shredded lettuce.

- 1 large orange
  About 3 cups shredded iceberg lettuce
- 4 green onions, finely chopped
- 6 ounces sliced cooked ham, chicken or turkey breast, tongue, or rare roast beef
- 3 tablespoons olive oil or salad oil
- 1½ teaspoons white wine vinegar
- 2 teaspoons lime or lemon juice
- 1 clove garlic, minced or pressed
- ¼ teaspoon *each* sugar, chili powder, and ground coriander
- 1 small avocado, peeled, pitted, and sliced
  Pitted ripe olives

Cut peel and white membrane from orange and cut orange into thin slices; set aside. Mix lettuce with onions. Cut meat into julienne strips and mix half into greens. Stir together oil, vinegar, lime juice, garlic, sugar, chili powder, and coriander; pour dressing over greens and toss lightly. Mound in center of a rimmed platter (about 9 inches in diameter). Arrange remaining meat strips on top of greens. Arrange avocado and orange slices around base. Garnish with olives.

Tostada

⏱ *Preparation time (cooking included): 15 minutes*

Pile high this meaty Mexican salad and surround it with crisp tortilla chips.

½ **pound lean ground beef**
1 **small onion, chopped**
1 **can (8 oz.) red kidney beans, drained**
¾ **teaspoon chili powder**
¼ **teaspoon ground cumin**
3 **tablespoons catsup**
   About 3 cups shredded iceberg lettuce
½ **cup shredded jack cheese**
1 **medium-size tomato, cut in wedges**
   Tortilla chips

Crumble meat into an 8 or 9-inch frying pan, add onion, and cook, stirring, over medium heat until meat has lost its pink color and onion is limp; drain and discard excess fat. Add kidney beans, chili powder, cumin, and catsup; simmer gently, covered, for about 5 minutes to blend flavors.

Meanwhile, arrange lettuce on 2 dinner plates. Top lettuce with hot beef mixture, sprinkle with cheese, and garnish with tomato wedges and tortilla chips. Pass additional chips at table.

Roast Beef and Crab Salad

⏱ *Preparation time: 10 minutes. Chilling time: 15 minutes*

Rare roast beef and crab may seem like an odd couple, but they team up deliciously with creamy tarragon dressing, and the result is an unusual and filling salad.

For each serving, arrange outer leaves of **butter lettuce** on a plate; tear several additional leaves and mound in center of plate. Arrange 3 or 4 thin slices rare **roast beef** (about ¼ lb.) folded in half, several chunks of **crab meat** (about 2 oz.), 3 sliced **mushrooms,** 6 **cherry tomatoes,** ¼ cup canned **garbanzos,** ½-ounce chunk **blue cheese** or Roquefort (crumbled), and 3 **marinated artichoke hearts.** Cover and chill at least 15 minutes. Spoon over **tarragon dressing** (recipe follows). Makes 1 serving.

Tarragon dressing. Blend together ¼ cup *each* **sour cream** and **mayonnaise.** Stir in 1 tablespoon **lemon juice,** ¼ teaspoon crumbled **tarragon leaves,** and ⅛ teaspoon *each* **dry mustard** and **garlic salt.** Makes ½ cup.

Salmon Salad with Oranges

⏱ *Preparation time: 10 minutes*

Canned salmon goes together quickly with fresh orange sections and tangy sour cream dressing.

1 **can (about 8 oz.) salmon, drained**
1½ **cups thinly sliced celery**
⅓ **cup thinly sliced green onion**
2 **tablespoons finely chopped parsley**
¼ **cup thinly sliced pimento-stuffed green olives**
2 **large oranges**
   Tangy dressing (recipe follows)
   Lettuce leaves
   Sliced pimento-stuffed green olives

Turn salmon into a bowl, discard skin and bones, and break salmon into bite-size pieces. Add celery, onion, parsley, and the ¼ cup olives. Mix together lightly; chill for at least 15 minutes.

Just before serving, peel oranges and remove all white membrane. Separate orange sections and set a few aside for garnish; cut remaining sections in half and add to salmon.

Lightly toss salad with tangy dressing and serve on lettuce-lined plates. Garnish with reserved orange sections and sliced green olives.

(Continued on next page)

...Salmon Salad with Oranges (cont'd.)

Tangy dressing. Mix together 3 tablespoons *each* **sour cream** and **mayonnaise**, 1 teaspoon *each* **Dijon mustard** and **prepared horseradish**, ½ teaspoon **garlic salt**, ⅛ teaspoon **pepper**, and 1 teaspoon grated **orange peel.**

Hot Chicken Salad

⏱ *Preparation time (cooking included): 10 minutes*

For a light and low-calorie meal, serve this hot chicken salad adapted from a classic Chinese recipe. Add the warm and well-seasoned chicken at the very end to keep the lettuce crisp.

> 2 teaspoons *each* **sesame seeds, prepared mustard, and lemon juice**
> 2 tablespoons **regular-strength chicken broth or water**
> ¼ teaspoon *each* **salt, sugar, and ground coriander**
> ¼ cup **chopped green onion**
> 1½ cups **diced or shredded cooked chicken or turkey**
> About 2 cups **shredded iceberg lettuce**

Toast sesame seed in a frying pan over medium heat until golden, stirring frequently. Stir in mustard, lemon juice, chicken broth, salt, sugar, coriander, and onion. Add chicken and heat through. Arrange shredded lettuce on a warm platter and spoon hot chicken mixture over.

Tuna and Fruit Salad

⏱ *Preparation time (cooking included): 15 minutes.*
⏱ *Chilling time: 30 minutes*

A combination of shell macaroni, fruit, tuna, and toasted almonds tossed with a curry dressing makes a very special seafood salad.

> ½ cup **small shell macaroni**
> **Boiling salted water**
> 1 large **apple, cored and diced**
> 2½ tablespoons **lemon juice**
> 1 cup **sliced celery**
> ½ cup **raisins or halved seeded grapes**
> ¼ cup **thinly sliced green onion**
> 1 can (6½ oz.) **tuna, drained**
> ½ cup **mayonnaise**
> 1½ teaspoons **curry powder**
> 1 teaspoon **Dijon mustard**
> **Salt**
> ⅓ cup **sliced almonds**
> **Lettuce leaves**

Cook macaroni in boiling salted water as directed on package; drain and chill. Meanwhile, mix together apple, lemon juice, celery, raisins, onion, and tuna (breaking it apart with a fork).

Combine mayonnaise, curry powder, and mustard. Mix into salad gently; salt to taste. Cover and chill for at least 30 minutes.

Spread almonds in a shallow pan and toast in a 350° oven for 8 to 10 minutes or until golden; set aside.

Mix macaroni and half the almonds into salad. Serve salad on lettuce-lined plates with remaining almonds sprinkled on top.

Dilled Shrimp Salad

⏱ *Preparation time: 10 minutes. Marinating time: 1 hour*

Tiny pink shrimp marinate in a dill dressing. At the last minute you toss greens and cheese cubes with the shrimp and dressing—and there's dinner.

> 3 tablespoons **olive oil or salad oil**
> 2 teaspoons **white wine vinegar**
> 1 teaspoon **lemon juice**
> ¼ teaspoon *each* **dill weed and Dijon mustard**
> ⅛ teaspoon **salt**
> **Dash *each* garlic powder and pepper**
> ½ pound **small cooked shrimp**
> 1½ cups *each* **torn romaine and butter lettuce leaves**
> ¼ cup **cubed Tilsit or jack cheese**

pink inside. Let cool to touch. Discard skin and bones and cut meat into chunks—you should have about 2 cups.

Spread almonds in a shallow pan and toast in a 350° oven for 8 to 10 minutes or until golden; set aside.

Combine chicken, celery, onion, and green pepper. Grate ½ teaspoon orange peel; set aside. Remove remaining peel and white membrane, then thinly slice orange; cover and refrigerate. Blend sour cream, mayonnaise, sugar, lemon juice, reserved orange peel, and salt and pepper to taste. Stir into chicken mixture, cover, and chill for 2 to 3 hours.

To serve, place salad greens on individual serving plates; top with chicken mixture and garnish with reserved orange slices and almonds.

Vegetable Antipasto Salad

Preparation time (cooking included): 30 minutes. Chilling time: 2 hours

Traditionally served as appetizers, colorful antipasto vegetables can also become a tempting, chilled, whole-meal salad—appropriate for lunch or a light supper. Cooked just long enough to absorb an herb-flavored tomato sauce, the crisp vegetables are accompanied by sardines and hard-cooked egg wedges.

- 1 cup tomato-based chili sauce
- ¼ cup *each* olive oil and lemon juice
- 1 teaspoon *each* oregano leaves and prepared horseradish
- 1 clove garlic, minced or pressed
- 2 stalks celery, cut in ¾-inch-wide chunks
- 1 large green pepper, seeded and cut in ½-inch-wide strips
- 2 medium-size zucchini, cut in ¼-inch-thick slices
- 1 jar (8 oz.) peperoncini
   Lettuce leaves
   Sliced pimento-stuffed green olives
- 2 hard-cooked eggs, cut in wedges
- 1 can (3¾ oz.) sardines, packed in oil (drained)

In a wide frying pan, combine chili sauce, olive oil, lemon juice, oregano, horseradish, and garlic; cook for several minutes over medium heat.

Add celery, green pepper, zucchini, and peperoncini; simmer, uncovered, until vegetables are fork tender (about 12 minutes), stirring often. Cover and chill 2 to 4 hours—vegetables should be cold.

Lift vegetables from sauce with slotted spoon and mound on 2 lettuce-lined plates. Top each with 2 tablespoons sauce and garnish with sliced olives. Arrange hard-cooked egg wedges and sardines along one side of each plate.

In a small jar, combine oil, vinegar, lemon juice, dill weed, mustard, salt, garlic powder, and pepper; shake well to blend. Pour over shrimp; cover and refrigerate for about 1 hour, or until serving time.

Mix shrimp mixture lightly with greens and cheese.

Creamy Chicken with Oranges

Preparation time (cooking included): 30 minutes. Chilling time: 2 hours

A mound of orange-flavored chicken chunks on a lettuce leaf are topped with thin slices of orange and toasted almonds. Accompany with crisp bread sticks.

- 1 large whole chicken breast (about 1½ lb.), split
   Boiling salted water
- ¼ cup slivered almonds, toasted (directions follow)
- ⅓ cup sliced celery
- 2 tablespoons *each* chopped green onion and green pepper
- 1 large orange
- ¼ cup *each* sour cream and mayonnaise
- 1½ teaspoons *each* sugar and lemon juice
   Salt and pepper
   Crisp salad greens

In a wide frying pan, place chicken breast in about 1 inch boiling salted water; cover, reduce heat, and simmer for about 15 minutes or until meat is no longer

Marinated Mushroom Salad

⏱ *Preparation time: 10 minutes. Marinating time: 1 hour*

By itself, this marinated fresh mushroom salad is filling enough to make a light meal. But when combined with a cup of soup, it's a dinner delight. Chunks of zesty blue cheese and crunchy walnuts sprinkled over make an attractive serving. (See photograph on page 34.)

- ¼ cup olive oil or salad oil
- 2 teaspoons dry basil
- ½ teaspoon salt
- ⅛ teaspoon *each* pepper and paprika
- 2 teaspoons Dijon mustard
- 4 teaspoons white wine vinegar
- 1 teaspoon lemon juice
- ½ pound mushrooms, sliced
- ½ cup thinly sliced green onion, including some green tops
- ¾ cup broken walnut pieces (optional)
   About 4 ounces blue cheese, coarsely crumbled
- 3 cups torn chicory (curly endive), romaine, or butter lettuce leaves
   About 6 cherry tomatoes, whole or halved

In a salad bowl, combine oil, basil, salt, pepper, paprika, mustard, vinegar, and lemon juice. Beat with a fork until blended. Mix in mushrooms and green onion; marinate at room temperature for about 1 hour or until serving time.

Mix in walnut pieces, blue cheese, chicory, and cherry tomatoes. Or serve mushrooms on a lettuce-lined plate and garnish with walnut pieces, blue cheese, and cherry tomatoes.

Swiss Cheese Vegetable Salad

⏱ *Preparation time: 10 minutes. Chilling time: 1 to 3 hours*

Let vegetables marinate an hour in the piquant Italian herb dressing before combining with matchstick-size Swiss cheese pieces. Serve for a summer brunch or light supper.

- 1 small can (8 oz.) garbanzo beans, drained
- 1 small can (8 oz.) red kidney beans, drained
   About ½ head cauliflower, sliced ½ inch thick (about 1¼ cups)
- 1 zucchini (about 6 oz.) sliced ⅛ inch thick
- 1 small mild red onion, thinly sliced
   Italian herb dressing (recipe follows)
- 4 to 6 ounces Jarlsberg, jack, or Swiss cheese

In a bowl, mix garbanzo beans, kidney beans, cauliflower, zucchini, and onion. Add Italian herb dressing and mix lightly. Cover and refrigerate for 1 to 3 hours.

Cut cheese in matchstick-size pieces and mix into salad before serving.

Italian herb dressing. In a jar, mix together well 6 tablespoons **olive oil** or salad oil, ¼ cup **red wine vinegar,** 1 small clove **garlic** (minced or pressed), ¾ teaspoon **salt** (or to taste), ½ teaspoon **sugar,** ½ teaspoon **Italian herb seasoning** (or ¼ teaspoon *each* oregano leaves and dry basil), and ¼ teaspoon **pepper.**

Peanut and Tofu-filled Pineapple Boats

⏱ *Preparation time: 20 minutes*

Tofu puffs and peanuts supply the protein in this salad. A pineapple shell holds the salad, all dressed up in a spicy peanut butter sauce. Look for deep-fried tofu puffs in Oriental markets.

- 1 large pineapple (4 to 5 lb.)
- 1 small cucumber, thinly sliced
- ¼ pound bean sprouts
- 2 tablespoons thinly sliced green onion
- ½ cup sliced canned water chestnuts
   About 1½ ounces Japanese-style deep-fried tofu puffs, cut in ¾-inch cubes, or 5 ounces Chinese-style tofu puffs
   Peanut sauce (recipe follows)
- ¼ cup coarsely chopped salted peanuts

Cut pineapple lengthwise through stem. With a grapefruit knife, cut around edge of each half, leaving sides about ½ inch thick. Lift out fruit, cut away core, and cut fruit in ¾-inch cubes to make about 2 cups. Drain shells.

Just before serving, drain pineapple cubes; mix together with cucumber, bean sprouts, onion, water chestnuts, tofu, and peanut sauce. Spoon into pineapple shells and sprinkle with peanuts.

Peanut sauce. Stir together ⅓ cup **chunk-style peanut butter,** 3 tablespoons firmly-packed **brown sugar,** ¼ to ½ teaspoon crushed **red pepper,** and ¼ cup **lemon juice.**

Niçoise Supper Salad

Preparation time: 10 minutes

This classic salad can be made in many ways. Tuna is skirted by tomato, olives, hard-cooked egg, and crisp vegetables. Then everything is dressed with anchovy. For variation, try stuffing Arab pocket (peda) bread with the salad makings for hearty sandwiches. (See photograph on page 26.)

> Butter lettuce
> 1 small can (6½ oz.) chunk-style tuna, drained
> 2 hard-cooked eggs, halved or quartered
> 1 large tomato, cut in wedges
> 1 small green pepper, seeded and slivered
> ½ medium-size mild red onion, cut in rounds
> 1 stalk celery, thinly sliced
> ½ cup pitted black or green olives, drained
> 4 large mushrooms, thinly sliced (optional)
> 1 jar (6 oz.) marinated artichoke hearts, drained
> Alfalfa sprouts (optional)
> Canned miniature corn on the cob, drained
> Anchovies, drained
> Niçoise dressing (recipe follows)
> Arab pocket bread (optional)

Line a rimmed platter with butter lettuce. Place tuna in center. Around it group eggs, tomato, green pepper, onion, celery, and olives. If you like, also add mushrooms, artichoke hearts, alfalfa sprouts, miniature corn on the cob, and anchovies. Just before serving, moisten evenly with about half the dressing, then pass remaining dressing to serve over. Or stuff Arab pocket bread halves with any ingredients above.

Niçoise dressing. Blend 2 teaspoons *each* minced canned **anchovies** and **Dijon mustard** with 3 tablespoons **wine vinegar** and 5 tablespoons **olive oil.**

Curried Egg and Shrimp-stuffed Tomatoes

Preparation time: 10 minutes. Chilling time: 20 minutes

Partially sliced tomatoes have nifty pockets for a stuffing of egg and shrimp. Decorate with toasted almonds.

> 1½ tablespoons mayonnaise
> ¼ teaspoon curry powder
> ⅛ teaspoon garlic salt
> Dash cayenne
> 2 hard-cooked eggs, chopped
> 1 tablespoon chopped green onion
> 2 tablespoons chopped celery
> ⅛ pound small cooked shrimp, coarsely chopped
> 1 tablespoon sliced or slivered almonds
> 2 medium-size firm, ripe tomatoes
> Lettuce leaves

Mix together mayonnaise, curry powder, garlic salt, cayenne, chopped eggs, green onion, and celery. Cover and chill up to 24 hours. Add shrimp just before ready to serve.

Spread almonds in a shallow pan and toast in a 350° oven for 8 minutes or until golden; set aside.

To peel tomatoes, dip in boiling water 45 seconds, rinse in cold water, and slip off skins. Cut out stems.

Cut each tomato into 4 or 5 slices without cutting all the way through to stem.

Place tomatoes on lettuce-lined salad plates. Gently open slices and fill with several spoonfuls egg-shrimp mixture. Cover and chill for at least 20 minutes. Sprinkle with toasted almonds.

Basic Salad Dressings

These two old favorite dressings will stay fresh in the refrigerator 2 to 3 weeks. Toss with your favorite salad greens.

Vinaigrette Dressing

Mash 2 hard-cooked **egg yolks** to a paste with ¼ cup **malt vinegar** or cider vinegar. Gradually blend in 6 tablespoons **salad oil.** Stir in 2 finely chopped **green onions** and add **salt** and **coarsely ground pepper** to taste; mix well. Makes about ¾ cup.

Creamy Louis Dressing

Stir together 1 cup **mayonnaise,** ⅓ cup **sweet pickle relish,** 3 tablespoons finely chopped **green pepper,** and ⅛ teaspoon **liquid hot pepper seasoning.** Whip ½ cup **whipping cream** until stiff; gently fold into mayonnaise mixture until thoroughly blended. Cover and chill. Makes about 2 cups dressing.

SANDWICHES

A sandwich can be anything tucked between, placed atop, or rolled inside bread slices, buns, tortillas, crisp rye crackers, Arab pocket bread, or even a paper-thin omelet. Being innovative is half the fun.

Lots of hearty open-faced and closed sandwiches, filling enough for any meal, are here to enjoy. Making them doesn't require lots of forethought, and you get all the credit for the imagination. Serve them alone or with soup or salad.

Tuna Sandwiches with Bean Sprouts

 Preparation time: 10 minutes

Fresh bean sprouts add crunch to a tuna spread that's great on toasted English muffins. With a pair of these and some raw vegetables, you're all set for Saturday lunch.

- 2 **English muffins**
  Butter or margarine
- 1 **cup bean sprouts**
- 1 **can (6½ oz.) tuna, drained**
- ¼ **cup mayonnaise**
- 2 **tablespoons minced parsley**
- ⅓ **cup chopped dill pickle**
- ¼ **cup e*ach* chopped green pepper and sliced green onion (including some tops)**
- 1 **hard-cooked egg, cut in slices**
  Dill pickle slices
  Radishes

Split and toast English muffins and spread with butter. Scatter bean sprouts over muffins.

Mix together tuna, mayonnaise, parsley, pickle, green pepper, and onion. Heap on top of bean sprouts. Top each sandwich with slices of hard-cooked egg. Garnish each plate with a dill pickle slice and some radishes. Makes 2 sandwiches.

Zucchini and Egg Sandwiches

Preparation time: 10 minutes

You can eat this as a closed sandwich or open-faced. Crisp zucchini and egg slices make it a satisfying, wholesome meal.

- 3 **tablespoons mayonnaise**
- 1 **clove garlic, minced or pressed**
- ¼ **teaspoon e*ach* salt, pepper, and prepared horseradish**
- 2 **small zucchini, thinly sliced**
  Butter or margarine
- 2 **to 4 slices pumpernickel, rye, or whole wheat bread**
  Butter lettuce leaves
- 2 **tablespoons thinly sliced green onion**
- 1 **hard-cooked egg, sliced**

Mix together mayonnaise, garlic, salt, pepper, and prepared horseradish until blended. Stir in zucchini.

If you'd like open-faced sandwiches, just butter one side of 2 slices of bread. On each buttered slice, lay lettuce leaf . Then spoon half the zucchini mixture over each sandwich and sprinkle each with half the green onion. Arrange half the hard-cooked egg slices on each. Serve open-faced or top with an additional slice of buttered bread for a closed sandwich. Makes 2 sandwiches.

Curried Tuna-Apple Sandwiches

 Preparation time: 10 minutes

Curry lifts "good old tuna" above the ordinary, especially with bits of crisp apple and raisins contributing sweetness. Toasted raisin bread is the ideal base for these open-faced sandwiches.

- ¼ **cup mayonnaise**
- ½ **teaspoon curry powder**
- ¼ **teaspoon garlic salt**
  Dash cayenne
- 1 **tablespoon lemon juice**
- 1 **can (6½ oz.) chunk-style tuna, drained**
- ¾ **cup chopped apple**
- ½ **cup finely chopped celery**
- ¼ **cup raisins**
- 2 **tablespoons thinly sliced green onion (including some tops)**
  Butter or margarine
- 4 **slices raisin bread or whole wheat bread**
  Alfalfa sprouts (optional)

Mix together mayonnaise, curry powder, garlic salt, cayenne, and lemon juice. Stir in tuna, apple, celery, raisins, and onion until blended.

Toast and butter bread; spread equal portions of tuna mixture over each sandwich, then sprinkle with alfalfa sprouts, if you wish. Makes 4 sandwiches or 2 servings.

Salmon Sandwiches with Egg

 Preparation time: 10 minutes

A knife-and-fork sandwich that's ready in minutes is this nourishing one made from canned salmon.

Cut 4 thin center slices from 2 **hard-cooked eggs** and reserve for garnish. In a bowl, chop remaining egg and combine with 2 tablespoons **mayonnaise.** Spread egg mixture on 2 slices **whole wheat bread.** Top egg with sprigs of **watercress.** Drain 1 can (about 7 oz.) **salmon;** discard skin and bones, break salmon into chunks, and arrange evenly over cress. Garnish with egg slices. Makes 2 sandwiches.

Smoked Salmon Sandwiches

 Preparation time: 10 minutes

Arrange slices of smoked salmon over crisp cucumber slices and cream cheese for a pumpernickel special.

- 1 **small package (3 oz.) cream cheese, softened**
- 1 **teaspoon lemon juice**
- 2 **slices pumpernickel bread**
- 12 **cucumber slices**
- 1 **package (3½ oz.) sliced smoked salmon**
  Chopped green onion

Mix together until blended the cream cheese and lemon juice. Spread cream cheese over pumpernickel bread. Arrange half the cucumber slices on each sandwich and top with equal amounts of the smoked salmon. Garnish salmon with chopped green onion. Makes 2 sandwiches.

Ham and Cheese with Coleslaw

 Preparation time (cooking included): 10 minutes

Sandwich and salad are all one when you top ham and melted cheese with a generous serving of coleslaw. Carrot curls and tomato wedges are the final touch.

For each sandwich, toast 2 slices **rye bread** or split and toast an English muffin; spread with **butter** or margarine and **prepared mustard** to taste. Top each

with a slice of cooked **ham** and a slice of **Cheddar cheese** (about 2 oz. of *each*) and place under broiler until cheese melts. Top generously with **coleslaw** (homemade or purchased) and garnish with **tomato wedges** and **carrot** curls. Makes 1 sandwich.

Egg Crêpe Sandwiches

 Preparation time (cooking included): 10 minutes

Eggs cook in a thin layer to form a crêpe, which you top with cheese and chili powder, then roll up and tuck inside a toasted bun.

Split 2 sandwich-size **French rolls** or hot dog buns, spread lightly with **butter** or margarine, and toast cut surfaces in a wide frying pan over medium heat. Remove from pan and keep warm.

Lightly beat together 3 **eggs**. Melt 1 teaspoon **butter** or margarine in pan over medium heat; tilt pan to coat bottom. Add half the beaten egg; quickly tilt pan to form a thin, even layer over bottom. Sprinkle ¾ cup shredded **Cheddar cheese** and 1 teaspoon **Mexican seasoning** or chili powder over egg. When egg is lightly browned on bottom, remove from heat. With a wide spatula, roll egg up, fold in half, and place in **French roll** (leave unfolded for hot dog bun). Repeat with remaining egg. Makes 2 sandwiches.

Roast Beef Mushroom Sandwich

 Preparation time: 10 minutes

A mushroom-laden sandwich of rare roast beef can be topped with tomato wedges and a spoonful of creamy blue cheese dressing, if you like. (See photograph on facing page.)

For each sandwich, lightly toast 2 slices **corn rye bread** or split French rolls and spread with **mayonnaise** and **Dijon mustard** to taste. Place toast slices side by side on plate and cover each with several **lettuce** leaves. Top evenly with about 3 ounces thinly sliced rare **roast beef.** Sprinkle over meat 2 or 3 thinly sliced raw **mushrooms** and 2 to 3 thin slices of

A PORTABLE SOUP AND SANDWICH supper: quick gazpacho served in chilled mugs (page 5) and a roast beef sandwich stacked high with meat, sliced mushrooms, onion rings, and tomato wedges (recipe above). Finish meal with individual raspberry tarts (page 77).

mild onion, separated into rings. Season with **salt** and **pepper,** and garnish with **tomato wedges** and **ripe olives.** Spoon over **blue cheese dressing** or Italian-style dressing, if you wish. Makes 1 sandwich.

Toasted Jack Cheese and Mushroom Sandwiches

 Preparation time (cooking included): 10 minutes

Sautéed mushrooms, tomatoes, and cheese top this open-faced sandwich. Serve it hot from the broiler with a cup of onion soup for a quick lunch or supper.

About 3 tablespoons butter or margarine
½ pound mushrooms, sliced
4 slices light rye bread
2 medium-size tomatoes, peeled and sliced
6 ounces jack cheese, sliced
Parsley sprigs

In a wide frying pan over medium heat, melt 2 tablespoons of the butter; add mushrooms and cook until liquid evaporates. Toast bread, butter lightly, place on a baking sheet, and cover each slice with a layer of mushrooms, reserving ⅓ of them for garnish. Evenly arrange a layer of tomatoes atop mushrooms; cover evenly with cheese. Broil about 4 inches from heat until cheese melts. Spoon over reserved mushrooms and garnish with parsley sprigs. Makes 4 sandwiches or 2 servings.

Chicken Supper Sandwiches

 Preparation time (cooking included): 30 minutes

You'll need a knife and fork to eat these towering open-faced chicken sandwiches. Accompany them with an assortment of crisp raw vegetables.

1 whole chicken breast (about 1 lb.)
Salted water
4 slices bacon
2 English muffins, split, toasted, and buttered
4 slices mild red onion
1 large tomato, peeled and cut into 4 thick slices
½ cup shredded Longhorn Cheddar cheese

Simmer chicken in a small amount of salted water until meat is no longer pink throughout (about 15 minutes); drain, discard skin and bones, and slice meat.

(Continued on next page)

Meanwhile cut bacon slices in half crosswise and partially fry bacon to remove most of the drippings (bacon should still be limp). Drain well and set aside.

Distribute chicken evenly over muffin halves; top each with 1 onion slice and 1 tomato slice. Distribute cheese evenly over each and top each with 2 pieces bacon. Broil about 4 inches from heat until cheese is bubbly and bacon crisp (3 to 5 minutes). Four sandwiches serve 2.

Parmesan Scrambled Egg Sandwiches

 Preparation time (cooking included): 15 minutes

That any-time-of-the-day-or-night favorite—scrambled eggs with bacon—takes a turn as a sandwich filling.

Lightly **butter** both sides of 4 slices **whole wheat bread.** Toast both sides of bread in a wide frying pan over medium heat. Remove from pan and keep warm.

Lightly beat together 2 **eggs,** 2 tablespoons *each* chopped **parsley** and freshly cooked or canned **bacon crumbles** (or bacon-flavored vegetable protein chips), ¼ cup grated **Parmesan cheese,** and 2 teaspoons **instant minced onion.** Melt 1 tablespoon **butter** or margarine in pan. Pour egg mixture into pan and stir gently until cooked to your liking. Divide evenly between 2 slices of toasted bread. Top with remaining slices. Makes 2 sandwiches.

Elegant Asparagus Cheese Puffs

 Preparation time (cooking included): 20 minutes

There's something special about asparagus. Arranged with ham slices under a blanket of cheese, which puffs up as it's broiled, asparagus brings a touch of class to this sandwich. Serve with soup for a spring brunch or lunch.

    ½ pound asparagus or 1 can (8 oz.) asparagus
         spears
    2 slices firm white or wheat bread
         Boiling salted water
    4 ounces Swiss cheese, shredded
    1 tablespoon mayonnaise
 1½ teaspoons Dijon mustard
    ⅛ teaspoon prepared horseradish
 1½ tablespoons butter or margarine
    2 thin slices cooked ham, 3 to 4 inches square

Trim asparagus so tip ends fit bread slices; save remaining green ends for other uses. If using fresh asparagus, rinse tips well, then immerse in 1½ inches rapidly boiling salted water in a wide frying pan. Cook, uncovered, just until fork tender (5 to 7 minutes); drain well. If using canned asparagus, heat in its liquid until warm through; drain well.

Combine cheese, mayonnaise, mustard, and horseradish.

Spread butter evenly over both sides of each bread slice. In a wide frying pan over medium heat, toast bread until golden brown on both sides; arrange on a rimmed baking sheet. Top each bread slice with a slice of ham; arrange asparagus evenly on top, then evenly spread cheese mixture over all to completely enclose asparagus.

Broil about 6 inches from heat until cheese mixture browns. Makes 2 sandwiches.

Turkey, Avocado, Bacon Sandwich

 Preparation time (cooking included): 15 minutes

Quite a few of your favorite things get together to make this sandwich-and-salad supper. The crowning touch is a velvety dressing of Green Goddess.

For each serving, cook 3 slices **bacon** in a frying pan over medium heat until crisp; drain. Split a large soft **sandwich roll** and toast cut sides, or toast 2 slices firm white bread. Spread with **butter,** margarine, or

until liquid evaporates. Add butter and stir until melted, then cook until shallots are soft. Whirl egg yolks in blender, then gradually add butter mixture in a slow, steady stream; sauce will thicken. Chill until ready to use.

Thinly slice beef fillet. Spread each bread slice generously with chilled béarnaise sauce; top with slices of beef, add salt to taste, and cover with remaining bread slices, enclosing beef in béarnaise. Cut each sandwich in 2 or 3 easy-to-handle portions. For picnicking, wrap in plastic wrap and chill until time to serve. Makes 2 sandwiches.

mayonnaise. Place side by side on a plate and top evenly with 3 to 4 ounces thinly sliced cooked **turkey** or chicken breast, 2 or 3 thinly sliced **radishes,** the bacon, and several slices of **avocado.** Pile about ½ cup shredded **lettuce** on the side and sprinkle with **green onion** slices. Season with **salt** and **pepper** and garnish with **cherry tomatoes.** Pass **Green Goddess** or blue cheese dressing to serve over. Makes 1 sandwich.

Béarnaise and Beef Fillet Sandwiches

🕐 *Preparation time (cooking included): 20 minutes*

For an elegant picnic or candlelight supper, treat yourselves to thin slices of fillet of beef smothered in béarnaise sauce. Consider creamy mushroom soup (page 4) as a starter, accompanied by champagne.

 ¼ **cup red wine vinegar**
 ½ **cup minced shallots or mild red onion**
 ½ **teaspoon tarragon**
 ½ **cup butter or margarine**
 2 **egg yolks**
 ½ **to 1 pound hot or cold cooked beef fillet, trimmed of fat and thinly sliced**
 4 **slices firm-textured whole wheat bread or white bread**
   Salt

To make béarnaise sauce, simmer wine vinegar, shallots, and tarragon in a small pan over medium heat

Quick Sloppy Joes

🕐 *Preparation time (cooking included): 15 minutes*

Pickle relish gives a sweet, spicy flavor to this speedy version of an old favorite.

 ¼ **teaspoon salt**
 ½ **pound lean ground beef**
 1 **small onion, chopped**
   Dash pepper
 ½ **can (6-oz. size) tomato paste**
 ⅓ **cup water**
 ¼ **cup sweet pickle relish**
 2 **hamburger buns, split and toasted**

Sprinkle salt in a wide frying pan over medium-high heat; crumble ground beef into pan, add onion, and cook, stirring, until meat is browned and onions are limp (about 5 minutes). Drain and discard any fat. Stir in pepper, tomato paste, water, and pickle relish. Reduce heat and simmer, uncovered, for 1 to 2 minutes or until heated through. Spoon meat mixture over toasted buns. Makes 2 sandwiches.

Marinated Mushroom Sandwiches

🕐 *Preparation time: 10 minutes. Marinating time: 1 hour*

A garden-fresh sandwich pairing mushrooms with Swiss cheese, this one is most easily eaten with a knife and fork.

Stir together 3 tablespoons **olive oil,** 1 tablespoon **lemon juice,** and ¼ teaspoon *each* **garlic salt** and **oregano leaves.** Stir in ¼ pound **mushrooms** (thinly sliced through stem) and ⅓ cup thinly sliced **celery.** Cover and chill, stirring occasionally, for 1 hour or until serving time.

Butter 2 or 4 slices **rye bread.** On each of 2 slices, lay 1 leaf **butter lettuce,** then 1 or 2 slices **Swiss**

cheese. With a slotted spoon, lift mushroom mixture from dressing, let drain briefly, and mound ½ the mixture on each sandwich. Serve open-faced or top each with a slice of bread. Makes 2 sandwiches.

Sausage, Olive, and Artichoke Pizza

⏱ *Preparation time: 1 to 1¼ hours.*
Cooking time: 15 to 20 minutes

Crumbled Italian sausage flavors the quick, fresh-tasting sauce that tops our hearty pizza. Total preparation time is only about an hour—the dough for the crust needs to rise only once before shaping, and you can make the sauce while it's rising. (See photograph on facing page.)

For a change of pace, use the same dough and sauce to make the individual pizza turnovers called *calzone.* A fresh fruit salad makes a refreshing accompaniment to either of these entrées.

1	**package active dry yeast**
½	teaspoon **sugar**
½	cup **warm water** (about 110°)
¼	teaspoon **salt**
1½	tablespoons **olive oil**
1⅓	cups **bread flour**
	Sausage-tomato sauce (recipe follows)
	Cornmeal
	Olive oil
2	tablespoons grated **Parmesan cheese**
1	jar (6 oz.) **marinated artichoke hearts,** drained well
1	can (2¼ oz.) **sliced ripe olives,** drained well
1½	cups (6 oz.) shredded **mozzarella cheese**

In a large bowl, sprinkle yeast and sugar over water; let stand for 5 minutes to soften. Add salt, the 1½ tablespoons oil, and 1 cup of the flour; mix until dough is elastic and pulls away from sides of bowl. Turn out onto a board or pastry cloth sprinkled with remaining ⅓ cup flour. Knead until dough is smooth and springy, with small bubbles just beneath the surface (5 to 10 minutes). Place dough in a greased bowl and turn over to grease top; cover and let rise in a warm place until doubled (45 to 60 minutes).

Meanwhile, prepare sauce. Grease an 11-inch pizza pan or a 10 by 15-inch baking sheet, then dust with cornmeal and set aside. Punch down dough. Roll out on a floured board to an 11-inch circle. Lift dough off board and place on prepared pan; brush lightly with oil. Spread sauce evenly over dough circle to within ½ inch of edge. Sprinkle with Parmesan cheese, then evenly top with artichokes and olives. Sprinkle with mozzarella cheese.

Bake on lowest rack in a 450° oven for 15 to 20 minutes or until crust is well browned. Let stand for 5 minutes, then cut in wedges.

Sausage-tomato sauce. Crumble ½ pound **mild Italian sausage** into a wide frying pan. Add 1 tablespoon **olive oil** and cook over medium-high heat, stirring frequently, until meat is no longer pink when cut. Add 1 **onion** (chopped) and 1 clove **garlic** (minced or pressed); cook until onion is soft. Add 1 can (about 15 oz.) **pear-shaped tomatoes** (break up with a spoon) and their liquid, ½ teaspoon **dry basil,** ¼ teaspoon **oregano leaves,** and ¼ cup **dry white wine.** Cook, stirring frequently, until juices have evaporated and sauce is thickened (about 10 minutes).

Sausage and Mushroom Calzone

Prepare dough as directed above for pizza. Set dough in a warm place to rise; then immediately make sauce, adding ½ cup chopped **green pepper** and ¼ pound **mushrooms** (thinly sliced) to sausage along with onion and garlic. Spoon sauce into a bowl and refrigerate until cool to the touch (about 30 minutes). Omit Parmesan cheese, artichoke hearts, and olives; increase mozzarella cheese to 2 cups and stir into cooled sauce.

Punch down dough and divide in half. On a lightly floured board, roll out each piece to a 9-inch circle. Brush surface of each circle lightly with olive oil. Spread half the filling over half of each dough circle. Fold plain half over filling; press edges together. Roll ½ inch of pressed edges up and over; then seal and crimp.

With a wide spatula, transfer turnovers to a greased, cornmeal-dusted 10 by 15-inch baking sheet. Prick tops with a fork in several places, then brush lightly with olive oil. Bake as directed above for pizza.

Crunchy Egg Sandwiches

⏱ *Preparation time: 10 minutes*

For a new twist to egg salad sandwiches, try combining bean sprouts and fresh edible-pod peas.

Stir together 2 tablespoons **mayonnaise,** ¼ teaspoon *each* **garlic salt** and **pepper,** and ¾ teaspoon **Dijon mustard.** Add 3 chopped **hard-cooked eggs;** mix to blend.

(Continued on page 24)

SAUSAGE, OLIVE, AND ARTICHOKE PIZZA (recipe at left) is hearty fare for two. Made from scratch, this entrée can be ready to serve in only one hour and 15 minutes. Try a refreshing spinach salad alongside.

Butter 2 or 4 slices **rye bread,** pumpernickel, or whole wheat bread. On each of 2 slices, lay 1 leaf **butter lettuce** or about ⅓ cup bean sprouts. Arrange 6 to 8 raw **edible-pod peas** (ends and strings removed) over lettuce and mound half the egg salad over each sandwich. Sprinkle each with about 2 teaspoons thinly sliced **green onion,** if desired. Serve open-faced or top with bread. Makes 2 sandwiches.

With a Sandwich Breakfast, You Get a Packaged Meal

Filled with meat and fruit, sandwiches can offer a fine solution to breakfast boredom. Because they make a neatly packaged meal that's quick to assemble and easy to eat, breakfast sandwiches appeal to hurried commuters. At the same time, they're a satisfying and nutritious start to the day.

Here are five sandwich suggestions to spark your creativity. You can vary the meats and fruits to suit individual tastes and to take advantage of leftovers you have on hand— there's no limit to possible combinations.

Smoked Sausage and Apple Sandwich

Split 2 fully cooked **smoked sausage links** lengthwise. Place in a small frying pan over medium heat and brown lightly on all sides, adding a little **butter** or margarine if necessary. Lift out sausage; discard any drippings.

Add to pan about 1 tablespoon **butter** or margarine and about ½ small **apple,** peeled and thinly sliced. Sprinkle lightly with **sugar** and **ground cinnamon.** Cook until apple is golden brown on all sides.

Split, toast, and butter 1 **bagel.** Arrange sausages on one half; top with apple and remaining bagel half. Makes 1 sandwich.

Bacon and Banana Sandwich

In a small frying pan over medium heat, fry 2 to 3 slices **bacon** until crisp; drain well. Toast 2 slices **whole wheat bread** or firm white bread. Spread 1 slice with about 2 tablespoons **chunk-style peanut butter** and arrange bacon over top. Peel 1 small **banana** and slice lengthwise; arrange on bacon. Spread remaining toast with your favorite **fruit jelly** or with butter or margarine and place jelly side down on top of banana slices. Makes 1 sandwich.

Chicken and Orange Sandwich

Toast 2 slices **raisin bread** or firm white bread. Arrange sliced **cooked chicken** or turkey on 1 piece of toast and cover with fresh **orange slices,** canned mandarin oranges (drained), or fresh peach slices. Spread generously with **spiced apple yogurt** or vanilla-flavored yogurt, seasoned to taste with **ground ginger** or chopped crystallized ginger. Top with remaining toast. Makes 1 sandwich.

Ham and Pineapple Sandwich

Generously spread 2 slices **rye bread** with **butter** or margarine. Place 1 to 2 ounces sliced **cooked ham** on unbuttered side of 1 piece of bread. Top with a fresh or canned **pineapple** slice (well drained); sprinkle lightly with **ground nutmeg** and **brown sugar,** then top with 1 to 2 ounces sliced **jack cheese.** Cover with remaining bread slice, unbuttered side down. Cook in a sandwich grill until cheese is melted and bread is toasted. Makes 1 sandwich.

Braunschweiger and Prune Sandwich

Toast 2 slices **raisin bread** or whole wheat bread. Generously spread each slice with **apple butter;** cover 1 slice with 2 to 4 slices (*each* about ¼ inch thick) **braunschweiger** or liverwurst, and arrange halved moist-pack **pitted prunes** or dried apricots on top. Then add **butter lettuce** leaves and remaining toast, apple butter side down. Makes 1 sandwich.

Ground Beef Reuben Sandwiches

⏱ *Preparation time (cooking included): 15 minutes*

Robust is the word for this ground beef version of the Reuben sandwich, which features also the traditional ingredients of Swiss cheese, sauerkraut, and rye bread.

   1 **can (8-oz. size) sauerkraut**
   ½ **pound lean ground beef**
   ½ **envelope (single-serving size) instant onion soup**
   1½ **teaspoons prepared mustard**
   ½ **teaspoon Worcestershire**
        Salad oil
   2 **tablespoons tomato-based chili sauce**
   2 **sandwich-size slices Swiss cheese**
   4 **slices Russian rye bread, toasted and buttered**

Turn sauerkraut into a wire strainer, rinse well with water, and drain thoroughly.

Meanwhile, combine ground beef, instant soup, mustard, and Worcestershire; mix well and shape into 2 oval patties, each ½ inch thick.

In a wide frying pan over medium-high heat, cook patties until done to your liking, turning to brown both sides and adding oil if needed. Top each patty with ½ the sauerkraut, drizzle with ½ the chili sauce, and top with 1 slice Swiss cheese. Cover pan and cook just until cheese melts (1 to 2 minutes).

Place each meat patty on a slice of toasted bread; top with another slice of toasted bread. Makes 2 sandwiches.

Monte Cristo Sandwiches

⏱ *Preparation time (cooking included): 15 minutes*

Powdered-sugar-coated Monte Cristo sandwiches are traditionally made with slices of turkey, ham, and Swiss cheese—with currant jelly to spoon over as they are eaten. A beautiful, special treat for brunch.

   4 **slices white bread**
        Mayonnaise
   4 **sandwich-size slices Swiss cheese, ⅛ inch thick**
   2 **slices cooked ham, ⅛ to ¼ inch thick**
   2 **slices cooked turkey, ⅛ to ¼ inch thick**
   1 **egg, slightly beaten**
   2 **tablespoons half-and-half (light cream) or milk**
        Dash salt
   2 **to 4 tablespoons butter or margarine**
        Powdered sugar
        Parsley
        Currant jelly

Spread one side of each bread slice with a thin coating of mayonnaise. On two of the bread slices, place 2 slices cheese and 1 slice *each* ham and turkey; top with remaining bread slices, mayonnaise side down. Trim crusts and filling to make edges even, if you like. Cut each sandwich in half.

Beat egg with half-and-half and salt, then dip sandwiches into egg mixture. Melt butter in a wide frying pan over medium-high heat; add sandwiches and toast on both sides until cheese melts. Dust with powdered sugar, garnish with parsley, and serve hot with currant jelly to spoon over. Makes 2 sandwiches.

Avocado-Beef Tortilla Pizza

⏱ *Preparation time (cooking included): 20 minutes*

An ingenious way to make a quick pizza is with Mexican flour tortillas. All you do is brush both sides of the tortilla with olive oil, pile on the toppings, and bake in a hot oven. The crusts are thin and chewy-crisp.

   ½ **pound lean ground beef**
   ¼ **teaspoon salt**
   1 **small clove garlic, minced or pressed**
   ⅛ **pound mushrooms, sliced**
   2 **tablespoons green chile salsa**
   2 **large flour tortillas (about 8-inch size)**
        Olive oil or salad oil
   ¼ **cup *each* chopped onion and green pepper**
   1 **can (2¼ oz.) sliced ripe olives, drained**
   ¼ **pound jack or Mozzarella cheese, shredded**
   ¼ **cup grated Parmesan cheese**
   1 **small avocado, peeled, pitted, and cut into thin slices**
   ½ **cup sour cream**

Crumble beef into a wide frying pan and stir over medium heat until lightly browned; drain and discard fat. Add salt, garlic, mushrooms, and chile salsa. Cook, stirring, over high heat until liquid has evaporated (about 3 minutes).

Brush tortillas lightly with olive oil on both sides, making sure edges are oiled; place slightly apart on a baking sheet. Spread meat mixture evenly over tortillas; then scatter onion, green pepper, and sliced olives evenly over tops. Sprinkle evenly with jack cheese, then Parmesan.

Bake in a 475° oven until cheese melts and browns slightly (about 7 minutes). Arrange avocado slices over pizza tops. Pass sour cream to spoon over. Makes 2 pizzas or 2 servings.

Quick Quesadillas

 Preparation time (cooking included): 20 minutes

Broiled cheese-stuffed *quesadillas* (keh-sah-*thee*-yas) add up to the Mexican equivalent of grilled cheese sandwiches—with flour tortillas taking the place of sliced bread. Combine with a quick green salad and marinated tomatoes.

- ¼ cup *each* shredded Cheddar and jack cheese
- 1 flour tortilla (about 8-inch size)
- 1 slice mild red onion, separated into rings (optional)
- 1 tablespoon chopped, seeded, canned California green chile (optional)
- About 2 teaspoons grated Parmesan cheese (optional)
- About 2 teaspoons butter or margarine, melted

Distribute Cheddar and jack cheese over half the tortilla to within ½ inch of edge; add onion and green chile, if used. Sprinkle with Parmesan, if desired. Fold tortilla over and brush top with melted butter. Turn over onto a baking sheet and brush second side with butter. Broil about 3 inches from heat until top is lightly browned (about 2 minutes). Turn over and broil until other side is browned and cheese is melted (about 2 more minutes). Serve immediately. Makes 1 quesadilla.

Quesadilla variations. To make spicier quesadillas, drizzle 1 tablespoon **taco sauce** over filling.

To substitute a different cheese, pick one that melts easily, such as **Swiss,** American, or teleme.

To make a meat filling, omit either Cheddar or jack; add 1 slice or about ¼ cup diced **cooked chicken,** turkey, ham, or beef.

Pocket Bread Sandwiches

 Preparation time (cooking included): 20 minutes

There's no limit to the savory combinations you can stuff into Arab pocket bread (sometimes called peda or pita bread). The flat, chewy rounds, when torn in half, form pockets that are perfect for neatly containing hot or cold sandwich fillings. You can enlarge the

HUMBLE TUNA gets all dressed up for a quick Niçoise supper salad. Combine tuna with both fresh and canned sliced vegetables before tossing with anchovy-flavored dressing (page 15). For variety, stuff salad into pocket bread halves and serve as sandwiches.

pockets by gently working them open with a fork or your fingers.

Spicy Beef and Raisin Filling

- 2 tablespoons slivered almonds
- ½ pound lean ground beef
- ½ small onion, chopped
- ¼ cup *each* tomato-based chili sauce and water
- 2 tablespoons raisins
- ⅛ teaspoon ground cinnamon
  Dash ground cumin
  Salt and pepper
- 2 Arab pocket breads, cut in half
- ½ cup shredded jack cheese
- 1 cup shredded iceberg lettuce
- 6 to 8 cherry tomatoes, halved

Spread almonds in a shallow pan and toast in a 350° oven for 8 to 10 minutes or until golden; set aside.

In a wide frying pan over medium-high heat, crumble in beef and cook until browned, stirring often. Add onion and cook until limp. Drain and discard fat. Mix in chili sauce, water, raisins, cinnamon, cumin, and salt and pepper to taste. Cook, uncovered, stirring often, until liquid has evaporated (about 5 minutes). Stir in almonds.

Spoon hot meat mixture into pocket bread halves and top evenly with cheese, lettuce, and tomato halves. Makes 2 sandwiches.

Middle Eastern Lamb Patty Filling

- ½ pound lean ground lamb
- ½ teaspoon ground cumin
- ¼ cup chopped onion
- ¼ teaspoon salt
- 1 egg
- 1 tablespoon fine dry bread crumbs
  Salad oil
- 2 Arab pocket breads, cut in half
  Tender inner romaine leaves
- 6 to 8 cherry tomatoes, halved
- ½ mild red onion, thinly sliced
- ½ cup unflavored yogurt

Mix together lamb, cumin, onion, salt, egg, and bread crumbs. Shape into balls, using 1½ tablespoons for each; then flatten balls into ½-inch-thick patties.

In a wide frying pan over medium-high heat, brown lamb patties on both sides, without crowding, until all are done to your liking. Add oil, if needed.

Evenly fill each pocket bread half with meat patties, romaine leaves, tomato halves, and onion slices. Pass yogurt to spoon into each sandwich. Makes 2 sandwiches.

MEATS

What could be easier than meat for two? Two steaks, two chops, two hamburgers ...simple! Not to mention boring!

Happily, you don't have to choose between that kind of repetition and the other kind—the kind that comes with endless leftovers. There is a good middle ground, and it's covered on the following pages, with rack of lamb and prime rib for two, pot roasts and other meats that have big taste but are small enough for two, stews in manageable quantities that cook in reasonable time, ethnic dishes such as moussaka and schnitzel, and meltingly good special-occasion meats like pork tenderloin with onion-apple cream. Beef, liver, veal, pork, lamb—they're all here. Of course there will be many times when you'll want to take the two-chops route, but it doesn't have to be a way of life.

Our recipes list quantities of meat to buy, but as a further help, we suggest the following:

Waste-free meats are good selections for two—boneless veal and ham, ground meats, liver, and stew meat are all excellent choices; plan on ½ to ¾ pound for two servings. When buying meats with some bone—steaks or roasts, for example—allow about 1¼ pounds for two. And with very bony cuts such as lamb or beef shanks, spareribs, or shortribs, you'll need about 2 pounds.

Prime Rib for Two

 Preparation time: 5 minutes. Freeze meat ahead. Cooking time: 1 hour and 15 minutes

A one-rib roast is the perfect size for two servings. First, freeze the roast. Then it goes straight to the oven, where the outside sears before the inside thaws, deliciously capturing meat juices. Two big potatoes do "book end" duty in the oven, then help round out the meal, which might well end with chocolate ice cream laced with Grand Marnier.

> 1 **rib of a standing rib roast (about 2½ lb.)**
> 1 **tablespoon salad oil or olive oil**
> 1 **small clove garlic, minced or pressed**
> 2 **large baking potatoes**

Wrap meat well and freeze until solid.

Combine oil and garlic; rub evenly over frozen meat. Stand roast, rib bone down, on a rimmed baking sheet or broiler pan between the 2 potatoes, placed like book ends. *Roast frozen; do not thaw.*

Roast, uncovered, in a 400° oven for 1 hour and 15 minutes for rare meat, 1 hour and 25 minutes for medium rare, 1 hour and 35 to 40 minutes for well done. If you wish, insert a meat thermometer through fat layer into center of roast, not touching bone, after it has cooked for about 1 hour, and continue cooking until meat is done to your liking (130° to 135° for rare). Let stand for about 5 minutes before carving.

Beef Shank Pot Roast

Preparation time: 10 minutes. Cooking time: 2 hours and 15 minutes

Choose a casserole with a tight-fitting lid for this midget pot roast. You might round out the menu with hot rolls and a fruit salad that doubles as dessert.

> 2 **meaty slices beef shank, cut 1½ inches thick (about 1½ lb.)**
> 1 **tablespoon all-purpose flour**
> 2 **single-serving-size packages instant onion soup**
> 1 **clove garlic, minced or pressed**
> ½ **cup dry red wine**
> 1 **cup water**
> 1 **teaspoon Worcestershire**
> ¼ **teaspoon thyme leaves**
> 6 **small white boiling onions**
> 3 **medium-size carrots, cut in about 1½-inch pieces**

Sprinkle meat with flour, shake off excess, and place in a 1½ to 2-quart casserole. Sprinkle evenly with onion soup mix and add garlic, wine, water, Worcestershire, and thyme. Cover tightly and bake in a 375°

oven for 1 hour. Remove from oven, turn meat over, and add onions and carrots, tucking them in around meat. Cover and continue baking for about 1 hour and 15 minutes or until meat and vegetables are tender. Skim any excess fat from broth.

One-person pot roast. Use 1 slice **beef shank** (about 12 oz.) cut 1½ inches thick; enough **flour** to coat lightly; 1 single-serving-size package **onion soup mix;** 1 small clove **garlic,** minced or pressed; ¼ cup **dry red wine;** ½ cup **water;** ½ teaspoon **Worcestershire;** ⅛ teaspoon **thyme leaves;** 3 small white **boiling onions;** and 2 small **carrots,** cut in 1½-inch pieces. Bake in a 1-quart covered casserole.

Beef with Chinese Cabbage

⏱ *Preparation time (cooking included): 30 minutes*

Here is a colorful one-dish meal that uses lots of greens and is sparing of calories. Stir-fry it in a wok or a wide frying pan. Before starting to cook, be sure to have all the ingredients prepared—and that includes the cooking sauce.

- ½ to ¾ **pound lean boneless beef (such as sirloin, top round, flank)**
- 1 **teaspoon cornstarch**
- 1 **tablespoon soy sauce**
- ½ **teaspoon minced or grated fresh ginger, or ¼ teaspoon ground ginger**
- ½ **small head celery cabbage (also called Chinese cabbage) or regular cabbage**
- 4 **tablespoons salad oil**
- 1 **clove garlic, minced or pressed**
- 1 **medium-size red or green bell pepper, seeded and cut in 1-inch squares**
  Cooking sauce (recipe follows)
- 2 **green onions, thinly sliced**

Trim off and discard excess fat from meat; cut meat in ⅛-inch-thick diagonal slices. Blend cornstarch and soy with ginger in a bowl; mix in meat and set aside.

Cut celery cabbage across in ¾-inch slices (or regular cabbage in ¾-inch wedges).

In a wide frying pan or wok over high heat, heat 2 tablespoons of the oil; add meat mixture. Stir and turn until browned (2 to 3 minutes); turn out into serving dish.

Reheat pan; add remaining 2 tablespoons oil. When oil is hot, put in garlic and green pepper; stir and cook for about 30 seconds. Add cabbage and continue to stir and cook for about 2 minutes or until cabbage is tender-crisp and bright green.

Return meat to pan, add cooking sauce, and cook, stirring, until mixture boils and thickens (about 2 minutes). Stir in green onions, then turn out into serving dish.

Cooking sauce. Mix together 1 tablespoon *each* **cornstarch** and **sugar** with ½ cup regular-strength **beef broth,** 1 tablespoon **soy sauce** or oyster sauce, and 1 tablespoon **dry sherry** or white wine.

Paprika Pot Roast

⏱ *Preparation time: 20 minutes. Cooking time: 2 hours and 15 minutes*

When you have some time to let a dish simmer away, try Hungarian-inspired pot roast. It takes a little over 2 hours and comes out melt-in-your-mouth tender. Serve accompaniments of sour cream and noodles.

- 2 **tablespoons butter or margarine**
- 1½ **pound bone-in beef chuck roast**
- 2 **small onions, sliced**
- 1 **teaspoon caraway seed**
- 1½ **teaspoons paprika**
- ¾ **teaspoon salt**
  Dash pepper
- ¾ **cup water**
- 1 **tablespoon all-purpose flour**
- ½ **cup sour cream**
  Hot cooked noodles

Melt butter in a frying pan over medium heat; add roast and brown on all sides; remove meat to platter. Add onions to pan and cook, stirring occasionally, over medium heat, until limp; then stir in caraway seed, paprika, salt, pepper, and water. Return roast to pan, cover, and reduce heat to low; cook until meat is fork tender (about 2 hours and 15 minutes).

Remove roast to a platter and keep warm. Skim off

and discard excess fat from pan juices. In a bowl, gradually stir ⅓ cup of the juices into flour until smooth; blend in sour cream. Stir this mixture back into juices in pan and cook until thickened; pour into serving bowl. Serve pot roast with noodles; pass sauce to spoon over servings.

Beef Stroganoff

 Preparation time (cooking included): 20 minutes

Quickly browned strips of beef blended with mushrooms and sour cream can be served over hot noodles or rice in minutes.

    1 pound beef chuck steak or roast
    2 to 3 tablespoons butter or margarine
    1 tablespoon salad oil
    ¼ pound mushrooms, sliced
    ¼ cup finely chopped onion
    ½ teaspoon *each* salt and Worcestershire
       Dash *each* paprika and pepper
    ½ cup sour cream
       Chopped parsley
       Hot cooked noodles or rice

Cut out and discard bone and fat; cut meat into thin bite-size strips. Heat 2 tablespoons of the butter with oil in a wide frying pan over medium-high heat until foamy. Add mushrooms and onion and cook, stirring, until golden; lift out and set aside.

Add remaining 1 tablespoon butter to pan. Add beef strips and cook over high heat, turning meat and shaking pan, just until browned. Remove pan from heat; stir in reserved mushroom-onion mixture, salt, Worcestershire, paprika, pepper, and sour cream. Return pan to low heat and cook, stirring constantly, just until sauce is heated through—do not boil. Sprinkle with parsley. Serve over noodles.

Sesame Steak

Preparation time (cooking included): 20 minutes

Toasted sesame seed butter enhances thick, tender steak, and it's also good spooned over baked or new potatoes cooked in their jackets. Serve with sliced tomatoes, a green vegetable, and your favorite tart fruit sherbet.

    1 large porterhouse steak, cut 1 inch thick, or
       other tender steak of your choice
       Salt and pepper
    2 teaspoons sesame seed
    ¼ cup butter or margarine
    1 clove garlic, minced or pressed

Slash at 1 to 2-inch intervals through outside layer of fat on steak just to, but not into, meat. Season steak with salt and pepper to taste and place on a rack in a broiler pan about 2 inches from heat. Broil until done to your liking (about 6 minutes per side for rare).

As steak cooks, toast sesame seeds by shaking them in a small pan over medium-high heat. When they are richly browned, add butter and garlic. When butter melts, remove from heat and let stand until steak is done.

Transfer meat to a serving platter and pour butter sauce over it. Serve immediately, cutting thin slanting slices across grain of meat. Spoon some of the sesame butter over each serving.

Sesame steak for one. Substitute a 6 to 8-ounce **boneless tender beef steak** from the rib or loin, cut 1 inch thick. Use 1 teaspoon **sesame seed**, 2 tablespoons **butter** or margarine, and 1 small clove **garlic**.

Steak and Onions, Austrian-style

 Preparation time (cooking included): 50 minutes

Plenty of onions, cooked slowly to sweetness, are an unbeatable addition to quickly cooked steak. Accompany with gingered carrots, spinach-stuffed mushrooms (page 64), and for dessert, flaky apple turnovers from the freezer. (See photograph on facing page.)

    1 tablespoon butter or margarine
    1 tablespoon salad oil
    2 large onions, thinly sliced and separated into
       rings
    1 small clove garlic, minced or pressed
    2 beef fillets or ¾ to 1 pound top sirloin steak
       (¾ inch thick), cut into 2 equal pieces
       Salt and pepper
    ¼ cup dry vermouth or regular-strength beef
       broth
       Chopped parsley (optional)

Heat butter and oil in a wide frying pan over medium-low heat. Add onion and garlic and cook, stirring occasionally, until onion is limp and golden (about 30 minutes). Increase heat to brown onion slightly; remove from pan.

(Continued on page 32)

SLOWLY SAUTÉED ONION RINGS crown pan-fried steaks, Austrian-style (recipe above). Spinach soufflé-stuffed mushroom caps (page 65) and gingered sesame carrots (page 64) make colorful and tasty side dishes.

Meanwhile, sprinkle steaks with salt and pepper. In same pan, over high heat, brown steak quickly on both sides adding a little more butter and oil, if needed; cook until meat is done to your liking (about 2½ minutes on each side for rare). Remove to a warm platter.

Add vermouth to pan; heat quickly to reduce liquid slightly, stirring up browned bits from pan. Reduce heat, stir in onion, and heat thoroughly. Spoon onion mixture over steak. Sprinkle with parsley, if desired.

Hawaiian Short Ribs

 Preparation time: 10 minutes. Cooking time: 2 hours

White or brown rice complements these baked short ribs with their sesame seed sauce. Add a green vegetable or crisp salad, and lime-drizzled papaya halves for dessert.

1½ **tablespoons sesame seed**
    About 2 pounds beef short ribs, cut in 2 to 3-inch lengths
 1 **small onion, sliced**
 ¾ **cup water**
 ¼ **cup soy sauce**
 2 **tablespoons packed brown sugar**
 1 **small clove garlic, minced or pressed**
 ⅛ **teaspoon** *each* **ground ginger and pepper**
 1 **small dried hot chile pepper, seeded and crushed**
 1 **teaspoon** *each* **cornstarch and water**

In a 2 to 3-quart ovenproof pan, toast sesame seed over medium heat until lightly browned, shaking pan often to toast evenly. Remove from heat and arrange ribs and onion on top of seeds.

Combine water, soy, brown sugar, garlic, ginger, pepper, and chile pepper; pour over meat. Cover and bake in a 400° oven for 2 hours or until meat is fork tender; stir well occasionally.

Lift meat to a warm serving dish; keep warm. Skim fat from pan juices. Combine cornstarch and water, stir into juices, and cook, stirring, until thickened; pour over meat.

winner even with those who usually say no thanks to liver. Consider serving carrots with sesame seed (page 64) and a salad of grapefruit and avocado slices with oil and vinegar dressing.

 ¾ **pound liver, cut in ½-inch-thick slices**
    Salt, pepper, and all-purpose flour
 1 **egg, slightly beaten**
 ⅓ **cup saltine cracker crumbs**
 ¼ **cup butter or margarine**
 2 **tablespoons lemon juice**
 ½ **teaspoon sugar**

Sprinkle liver slices with salt and pepper, then coat lightly with flour; shake off excess. Dip each floured liver slice into beaten egg, then into cracker crumbs until evenly coated. Melt 2 tablespoons of the butter in a wide frying pan over medium-high heat. Cook liver slices quickly until nicely browned on both sides and juicy-pink inside (about 3 to 4 minutes total).

Remove liver to a serving plate and keep warm. Melt remaining 2 tablespoons butter in pan, add lemon juice and sugar, and stir until sugar is dissolved. Pour sauce over liver and serve.

Liver in Lemon Butter

 Preparation time (cooking included): 20 minutes

Liver is an economical choice for a main dish for two. Cooked briefly to keep the meat juicy and pink inside, then served with a sprightly lemon butter, this dish is a

Liver Provençale

 Preparation time (cooking included): 15 minutes

Garlic and herbs flavor another quick-cooking liver entrée. Accompany it with buttered green beans and a robust salad with an oil and vinegar dressing.

- ¾ **pound liver, cut in ½-inch-thick slices**
  Salt, pepper, and all-purpose flour
- 1 **tablespoon butter or margarine**
- 1 **tablespoon salad oil**
- 1 **large clove garlic, minced or pressed**
- ⅛ **teaspoon dry rosemary, crumbled**
- ¼ **cup regular-strength beef broth**
  Chopped parsley

Cut each slice of liver in ½ to 1-inch-wide cross-grain strips. Sprinkle with salt and pepper, then coat with flour, shaking off excess. Heat butter and oil in a wide frying pan over medium-high heat. Add garlic and liver. Brown liver well on 1 side (about 2½ minutes), then turn and sprinkle with rosemary. Continue cooking for about 2½ minutes longer or until browned but still slightly pink inside when slashed. Remove liver to a warm serving dish.

Add broth to pan and cook, stirring up browned bits, until liquid is reduced by about half. Pour over liver. Sprinkle with parsley.

Top Round with Mushrooms

⏱ *Preparation time: 20 minutes. Marinating time: 2 hours*

Slowly marinated, then quickly broiled or grilled, round steak becomes as tender and full of flavor as a more expensive cut of beef. Mushrooms, cherry tomatoes, and green onions are the crowning touch.

- ½ to ¾ **pound top round steak**
- ¼ **cup *each* salad oil and chopped onion**
- 2 **tablespoons white wine vinegar**
- ¼ **teaspoon *each* salt and oregano leaves, crumbled**
  Dash pepper
- 2 **tablespoons butter or margarine**
- ¼ **pound sliced mushrooms**
- ½ **cup halved cherry tomatoes**
- 2 **green onions, sliced (include some green tops)**

Place steak in a shallow baking dish. Mix together oil, onion, vinegar, salt, oregano, and pepper; pour over steak. Cover and refrigerate for several hours, turning meat occasionally.

Melt butter in a wide frying pan over medium heat. Add mushrooms and cook until liquid evaporates; keep warm.

Remove steak from marinade, drain briefly, and place on rack in broiler pan or on a grill about 4 inches from heat. Cook for about 4 minutes on each side for rare to medium-rare, basting often with marinade.

To serve, top steak with mushrooms. Slice meat in thin diagonal slices across the grain. Garnish with tomatoes and green onion slices.

Ground Beef Burgundy

⏱ *Preparation time (cooking included): 15 minutes*

Ground beef takes the place of beef chunks in this variation of the traditional French boeuf bourguignon. It goes together quickly with supplies from your kitchen shelf.

- ½ **pound lean ground beef**
- 1½ **teapoons all-purpose flour**
- ½ **cup dry red wine**
- 1 **tablespoon instant minced onion**
- 1 **can (2 oz.) sliced mushrooms, drained**
- ¼ **teaspoon thyme leaves**
- ¼ **bay leaf**
- 1 **clove garlic, minced or pressed**
- 1 **tablespoon chopped parsley**
  Hot cooked rice or noodles

In a wide frying pan over medium-high heat, cook beef until crumbly. Stir in flour and cook until it browns slightly. Add wine, instant onion, mushrooms, thyme, bay leaf, and garlic. Simmer, uncovered, stirring occasionally, for about 5 minutes or until liquid is slightly reduced. Remove bay leaf and turn meat mixture into a serving dish; sprinkle with chopped parsley. Serve over rice or noodles.

Beef and Avocado Loaves

 Preparation time: 15 minutes. Cooking time: 15 minutes

Avocado and cheese are the surprise stuffing in these plump individual meat loaves. Tortilla chips, sliced tomatoes, and beer or dry red wine round out the meal nicely.

- ¾ pound lean ground beef
- 3 tablespoons fine dry bread crumbs
- ½ cup tomato-based chili sauce
- 1 egg
- ¼ cup finely chopped onion
- ½ teaspoon salt
- ⅛ teaspoon pepper
- 1½ teaspoons Worcestershire
- ½ cup shredded jack cheese
- 2 tablespoons seeded and diced canned California green chiles
- 1 small avocado, peeled, pitted, and halved

Mix together ground beef, bread crumbs, ¼ cup of the chili sauce, egg, onion, salt, pepper, and Worcestershire. Divide mixture into 4 equal portions and flatten each into an oval patty about 5 inches long. Combine cheese and 1 tablespoon of the green chiles; stuff evenly into avocado halves and place each, cheese side down, on a beef patty. Top with remaining patties and pinch together to enclose avocado. Place, flat side down, on a rimmed baking sheet.

Bake in a 375° oven for 15 minutes or until meat is barely pink when slashed. Meanwhile, combine remaining ¼ cup chili sauce with remaining 1 tablespoon green chiles; heat. Pass in a bowl to spoon over meat.

Mushroom-Raisin Meat Loaf

 Preparation time: 5 minutes. Cooking time: 1 hour

Here's a loaf that can pass for a French terrine. Serve hot for dinner, or chill it and take it on a picnic to slice and serve on firm-textured bread. Bacon slices decorate the top and add flavor to the spicy meat mixture. (See photograph on facing page.)

AN ELEGANT PICNIC: slices of mushroom-raisin meat loaf (recipe above); mugs of chilled, makeahead curried broccoli soup (page 4); marinated mushroom salad sprinkled with chunks of zesty blue cheese (page 14); and fresh raspberries and cream cheese to spread on firm ginger cookies.

- ½ cup fine dry bread crumbs
- ¾ pound lean ground beef
- ¼ pound bulk sausage
- 1 egg
- 1 tablespoon nonfat dry milk
- 2 tablespoons raisins
- ¼ pound mushrooms, coarsely chopped
- 1 tablespoon Worcestershire
- ¼ teaspoon *each* salt and pepper
- 2 strips bacon, cut in half
- 2 tablespoons catsup

Mix together crumbs, ground beef, sausage, egg, dry milk, raisins, mushrooms, Worcestershire, salt, and pepper. Press lightly into a 1-quart baking dish, tureen, or loaf pan. Lay bacon strips lengthwise on loaf and drizzle with catsup. Bake, uncovered, in a 350° oven for 1 hour or until meat is no longer pink inside when slashed.

Flaming Veal Amandine

 Preparation time (cooking included): 20 minutes

What could be more elegant and delicious than veal flamed in Marsala wine and bathed in an almond cream sauce? If time is of the essence, you can partially prepare the dish ahead, then finish it in minutes.

- ¾ pound boneless veal, cut about ½ inch thick
- 2 tablespoons butter or margarine
- ½ cup sliced or slivered almonds
  Salt
- 3 tablespoons Marsala wine or brandy
- 1 tablespoon lemon juice
- ⅓ cup whipping cream

Trim off and discard membrane from veal. Place meat between 2 sheets of wax paper and pound ¼ inch thick with smooth side of a mallet.

In a wide frying pan over medium heat, melt 1 tablespoon of the butter. Add almonds; cook, stirring, until golden; spoon nuts out of pan and set aside. Melt 1 more tablespoon of the butter over high heat. Sprinkle meat lightly with salt and cook, without crowding, until meat is lightly browned on each side. Set meat aside as it cooks; add more butter to frying pan, if needed.

When all meat is cooked, return it and any juices to frying pan. Add Marsala and set aflame at once (*not under an exhaust fan or flammable items*), shaking pan until flames subside. Pour lemon juice over meat, then lift meat from pan and arrange in a serving dish; keep warm. (If cooked ahead, place pieces of meat side-by-side in a shallow rimmed pan, cover, and chill. To reheat, uncover and place in a 375° oven for 3 to 4 minutes while preparing sauce.)

(Continued on next page)

Pour cream into frying pan. Boil rapidly, stirring, until large shiny bubbles form over entire surface and cream is a rich golden color; drain any juices from meat into sauce. Stir in almonds and spoon sauce over meat; serve at once.

Veal Piccata

 Preparation time (cooking included): 20 minutes

For a last-minute dinner that's out of the ordinary, cook lemony veal piccata strips and serve with buttered broccoli spears.

- ¾ **pound boneless veal, cut ½ inch thick**
- 1 **tablespoon all-purpose flour**
- ½ **teaspoon salt**
- ⅛ **teaspoon pepper**
- 3 **tablespoons butter or margarine**
- ⅓ **cup dry white wine**
- 1 **teaspoon grated lemon peel**
  Lemon slices

Place meat between 2 sheets of wax paper and pound ¼ inch thick with smooth side of a mallet. Cut meat into strips about 1½ inches wide and 3 inches long. Mix together flour, salt, and pepper. Lightly dust meat with flour mixture, shaking off excess.

Melt 2 tablespoons of the butter in a wide frying pan over medium-high heat. Add meat and cook quickly, turning to brown both sides (takes about 4 minutes total).

Remove meat to a warm platter. To pan, add wine and bring to a boil, scraping up browned bits. Stir in lemon peel and remaining 1 tablespoon butter; heat until melted. Spoon sauce over veal and garnish with lemon slices.

Veal piccata for one. Pound 6 to 8 ounces **veal cutlet** as directed above. Sprinkle with **salt** and **pepper** and enough **all-purpose flour** to coat lightiy; shake off excess. Cook in 1 tablespoon **butter** or margarine. For sauce, use 3 tablespoons **dry white wine,** ½ teaspoon **lemon peel,** and 1½ teaspoons **butter** or margarine. Garnish with 2 thin **lemon** slices.

Veal Stew with Spring Vegetables

 Preparation time: 20 minutes. Cooking time: 1 hour and 30 minutes

This stew resembles the delicate French *blanquette de veau* or white veal stew—white because of the cream sauce it's served in. If you make it ahead, wait until you reheat it to add the egg yolk.

- 1½ **tablespoons butter or margarine**
- 1 **medium-size onion, finely chopped**
- 1 **small carrot, finely chopped**
- 1 **pound boneless veal stew meat, cut in 1-inch cubes**
- ¾ **cup water**
- ⅛ **teaspoon thyme leaves**
- ½ **bay leaf**
- ½ **teaspoon salt**
- ¼ **pound small whole mushrooms**
- ¾ **cup frozen peas, thawed**
- ⅓ **cup whipping cream**
- ½ **teaspoon cornstarch**
- 1 **egg yolk**

Melt butter in a wide frying pan over medium heat; add onion and carrot and cook, uncovered, just until vegetables are soft but not browned, stirring occasionally. Add veal and cook, covered, over medium-low heat, stirring occasionally, until meat loses pink color and releases juices. Add water, thyme, bay leaf, and salt; simmer, covered, for about 1½ hours or until meat is very tender when pierced.

With a slotted spoon, lift meat from juices and set aside. Discard bay leaf. Bring liquid to boiling and add mushrooms; cook rapidly, uncovered, for 5 minutes; then add peas and cook for 2 minutes more. Blend cream with cornstarch and add to boiling liquid, stirring until slightly thickened. Return meat to pan and heat through. Remove pan from heat. Stir a little of the hot liquid into egg yolk, then return to pan, stirring to blend. Serve in large soup bowls.

Schnitzel

 Preparation time (cooking included): 30 minutes

Golden veal cutlets and mushrooms topped with a sour cream wine sauce—that's what makes up this version of an Austrian classic.

- ½ **pound boneless veal, cut in ½-inch-thick slices**
- ½ **cup fine dry bread crumbs**
- ½ **teaspoon salt**
- ¼ **teaspoon pepper**
  About 3 tablespoons all-purpose flour
- 1 **egg beaten with 1 tablespoon milk**
- 5 **tablespoons butter or margarine**
- ¼ **pound mushrooms, sliced**
- 2 **tablespoons finely chopped onion**
- ½ **cup *each* dry white wine and regular-strength chicken broth**
- 2 **teaspoons paprika**
- ½ **cup sour cream**

Place meat between 2 sheets of wax paper and pound ¼ inch thick with smooth side of a mallet.

Combine bread crumbs, salt, and pepper. Dust cutlets with about 2 tablespoons of the flour, shake off excess, dip them into egg mixture, then into crumb mixture. In a wide frying pan, melt 4 tablespoons of the butter over medium heat and cook cutlets until golden (2 to 3 minutes on each side). Place on a platter and keep warm.

Add remaining 1 tablespoon butter to pan and cook mushrooms and onion until onion is limp. Add wine, broth, and paprika; bring to a rolling boil, scraping up browned bits from pan. Stir remaining 1 tablespoon flour into sour cream, then stir into broth mixture and cook until hot through and slightly thickened. Pour over cutlets and serve at once.

Veal Strips Sauté with Artichokes

🕐 *Preparation time (cooking included): 15 minutes*

For a little taste of Italy, accompany this quick sauté with green noodles and an antipasto-style salad of thinly sliced tomatoes, olives, and anchovies.

- ¾ **pound boneless veal, cut in ½-inch-thick slices**
- 2 **tablespoons all-purpose flour**
- ¼ **teaspoon salt**
- ⅛ **teaspoon** *each* **pepper and paprika**
- 1 **jar (6 oz.) marinated artichoke hearts, drained**
- 1 **medium-size onion, sliced**
  Butter or margarine
- ¼ **cup water or regular-strength chicken broth**
- 1 **tablespoon lemon juice**
- ½ **cup sour cream**
- 2 **tablespoons grated Parmesan cheese**
  Hot cooked green noodles

Trim all membrane from veal slices; place meat between 2 sheets of wax paper and pound ¼ inch thick with smooth side of a mallet. Cut each piece into ¾-inch-wide strips. Combine flour, salt, pepper, and paprika. Dredge meat in flour mixture, shaking off excess.

Drain artichoke marinade into a wide frying pan (reserve artichokes for garnish); cook over medium heat until bubbly. Add meat strips, a few at a time, and cook quickly, stirring, until well browned (3 to 5 minutes); lift out and set aside.

When all the meat is browned, add onion to pan with butter, if needed; cook onion until limp (about 5 minutes). Add water and stir to loosen browned bits. Stir in lemon juice, sour cream, cheese, and veal strips. Heat through (do not boil) and serve over noodles. Garnish with artichoke hearts.

Lamb, Persian-style

🕐 *Preparation time: 20 minutes. Cooking time: 1 hour and 10 minutes*

A tantalizing combination of subtly spiced lamb and fresh nectarine slices, this dish is enhanced by plain yogurt—you spoon it over both meat and fruit. Brown or white rice goes well with this. The meat cooks while you read the evening paper.

- 2 **teaspoons salad oil**
- ⅓ **cup chopped onion**
- ¼ **teaspoon salt**
  Dash pepper
- ½ **teaspoon** *each* **ground cinnamon and cloves**
- 2 **teaspoons sugar**
- ¾ **to 1 pound lean boneless lamb shoulder, cut in bite-size pieces**
- 1 **tablespoon lemon juice**
  About 2 tablespoons water
- 1 **large nectarine or peach**
- 1 **tablespoon butter or margarine**

Heat oil in a wide frying pan over medium-high heat. Add onion and cook, stirring, until limp. Then stir in salt, pepper, cinnamon, cloves, and sugar. Add meat, turning to coat with onion mixture. Add lemon juice and 1 tablespoon of the water; cover and simmer for about 1 hour and 10 minutes or until meat is fork tender. Stir occasionally during cooking, adding a little more water if needed. Discard any fat and turn meat into a serving dish.

Meanwhile, cut nectarine or peeled peach into thick slices. Heat butter in a small frying pan over medium heat. Put in fruit and cook, turning gently, just until heated through (about 3 minutes). Arrange on top of meat.

Lamb Kebabs

 Preparation time: 15 minutes. Marinating time: 4 hours. Heat coals: 35 minutes. Cooking time: 20 minutes

A tart lemon marinade accents these lamb kebabs—you'll want to plan ahead for overnight marinating. They're good with rice pilaf, stuffed eggplant (page 65), and well-chilled melon. (See photograph on facing page.)

- ¾ **to 1 pound lean, tender boneless lamb, cut in 1 to 1½-inch cubes**
  Lemon marinade (recipe follows)
- ½ *each* **small red and green bell pepper**
- ½ **small mild red or white onion (optional)**
- 4 **medium-size mushrooms**
- 2 **lemon slices**

Combine meat and marinade; cover and chill for 4 hours or until next day. Seed peppers and cut into 1 to 1½-inch squares. Cut onion, if used, into wedges; separate each into layers.

Remove meat from marinade and drain; reserve marinade. Onto a 12-inch skewer, thread 1 mushroom, then alternate meat with peppers and onion, if desired, using ½ of each and adding 1 lemon slice. Thread on 1 more mushroom. Repeat on second skewer.

To barbecue, place skewers on a lightly greased grill 3 to 4 inches above a bed of low-glowing coals. Cook, turning and basting with marinade, for about 20 minutes, until meat is browned on all sides and still slightly pink inside (cut a gash to test).

Lemon marinade. Combine 2 tablespoons chopped **parsley**, ⅓ cup **salad oil**, 1 tablespoon **soy sauce**, ½ teaspoon *each* **dry mustard** and **Worcestershire**, ¼ cup **lemon juice**, and 1 clove **garlic**, minced or pressed.

Spicy Barbecued Lamb Chops

 Preparation time: 10 minutes. Marinating time: 4 hours. Heat coals: 35 minutes. Cooking time: 15 minutes

Lamb chops marinate in a spicy concoction overnight, for barbecuing the next day. Another time, try this versatile marinade recipe for chicken.

- ⅔ **cup dry red wine**
- 2 **tablespoons olive oil or salad oil**
- 2 **cloves garlic, minced or pressed**
- ½ **teaspoon** *each* **salt and ground cumin**
- ¼ **teaspoon ground cinnamon**
- 2 **teaspoons cumin seed**
- ¼ **cup finely chopped onion**
- 2 **shoulder lamb chops, cut about ¾ inch thick**

In a shallow baking pan, stir together wine, oil, garlic, salt, ground cumin, cinnamon, cumin seed, and onion. Turn lamb chops in marinade to moisten all sides, then arrange in a single layer. Cover and refrigerate for at least 4 hours or until next day, turning chops over in marinade occasionally, if possible.

To barbecue, remove chops from marinade and drain; reserve marinade. Place chops on a grill about 6 inches above a bed of hot-glowing coals. Cook, turning occasionally and basting often with marinade, until meat is done to your liking (about 15 minutes total for medium-well).

Grilled Lamb Steaks

 Preparation time: 15 minutes. Marinating time: 4 hours. Heat coals: 35 minutes. Cooking time: 12 minutes

For this dish, the longer the lamb marinates, the better the flavor—plan on 6 hours, at least. The best way is to marinate it overnight for barbecuing the next day. Fresh broccoli spears laced with butter are a good accompaniment.

- 2 **lamb leg steaks (about 1 lb.), cut about ¾ inch thick**
- ½ **cup cold strong coffee**
- ¼ **cup firmly packed brown sugar**
- 1 **tablespoon prepared mustard**
- ½ **teaspoon Worcestershire**
- 2 **tablespoons lemon juice**
  Dash liquid hot pepper seasoning
- 1 **clove garlic, minced or pressed**

Place steaks in a single layer in a shallow baking pan. Combine coffee, sugar, mustard, Worcestershire, lemon juice, hot pepper seasoning, and garlic; mix well and pour over lamb. Cover and chill for 4 hours or until next day. Turn steaks several times, if possible.

To barbecue, remove steaks from marinade and drain; reserve marinade. Place steaks on a grill about 4 inches above a bed of hot-glowing coals. Grill, basting often with marinade, until nicely browned on both sides (about 12 minutes total for medium-well).

IN THIS MIDDLE-EASTERN inspired barbecue, kebabs of lamb chunks, whole mushrooms, red and green pepper, and lemon (recipe above left) cook on a grill. Accompany entrée with stuffed eggplant halves (page 65), Armenian cracker bread, tall glasses of apricot nectar, and fruit and baklava for dessert.

Three Ways to Use Leg of Lamb

When you cook for just two, a whole leg of lamb—though certainly appealing—may seem a bit unwieldy. But with the help of your butcher, the leg can be divided into easily handled portions that you can use for three different mouth-watering entrées.

After selecting a full-cut leg of lamb, ask the meat cutter to first saw off four slices, each about an inch thick, from the large end (sirloin section). This gives you two hip blocks for a quickly assembled lamb chop *cassoulet*, and two leg steaks to pan-broil.

Then have him bone the remainder of the leg, cutting off the small shank end (about 1 lb.) for use in lemon-accented braised lamb stew. The center cut can be rolled and tied for an oven roast, which will give you a hearty dinner with plenty of cooked meat left over—use it for curried lamb another night; there may still be enough left for lamb sandwiches.

Generally, meat market personnel will do the cutting and boning without charge while you wait; some may require a day or two of notice. Once you have the meat home, cook the dishes in any order you choose; wrap and freeze the remaining cuts until needed.

Lamb Chop Cassoulet

Cut 2 strips **bacon** into 1-inch pieces; cook in a small frying pan over medium heat until lightly browned. Pour off all but about 2 tablespoons of the drippings and add 1 medium-size **onion,** sliced, and 1 clove **garlic,** minced or pressed; cook until onion is limp.

In a shallow 1½-quart baking dish, combine 1 can (15 oz.) **cannellini** (white kidney beans) and their liquid, the bacon mixture, 1 teaspoon **beef stock base,** 1 tablespoon tomato-based chili sauce, ¼ cup chopped **parsley,** and 1 **Polish sausage** cut in ¼-inch slices. On top, place 2 **hip-block lamb chops** (about ¾ lb. total). Cover and bake in a 375° oven for 30 minutes; remove cover and bake for 10 to 15 minutes longer or until chops brown lightly. Remove from oven and skim fat from juices. Reset oven to 400°.

Meanwhile, melt 1 tablespoon **butter** or margarine in a small frying pan. Add 1 slice **firm white bread,** crumbled, and stir until well coated; spoon over casserole. Continue to bake, uncovered, in a 400° oven for 10 minutes or until crumbs are crisp and brown.

Braised Lamb in Lemon Sauce

Trim excess fat from about 1 pound **boneless lamb** (the shank end and trimmings); cut meat into 1-inch pieces. Heat 1 tablespoon **salad oil** in a 3-quart pan over medium heat; add meat and brown well on all sides.

Stir in 1 medium-size **onion,** sliced, and 1 clove **garlic,** minced or pressed; cook until onion is limp. Add ½ teaspoon **oregano leaves,** dash of **pepper,** 1 **beef bouillon cube,** and ¾ cup **water.** Bring to boiling, reduce heat, cover, and simmer for 50 minutes or until meat is fork tender. Add 1 *each* medium-size **zucchini** and **crookneck squash,** thinly sliced. Cover; simmer for 6 to 8 minutes or until vegetables are fork tender.

With a slotted spoon, transfer meat and vegetables to a warm serving dish.

Beat 1 **egg** and ½ teaspoon **cornstarch** until blended; stir in 1 tablespoon **lemon juice.** Gradually stir hot cooking liquid into egg mixture. Return to pan and cook over low heat, stirring, until sauce thickens. Season with **salt** and **pepper** to taste, then pour over meat and vegetables. Garnish with 1 thinly sliced **green onion.**

Rolled Herbed Lamb Roast

Mix together 2 cloves **garlic,** minced or pressed; 1 tablespoon **dry vermouth;** 2 tablespoons **Dijon mustard;** and 1 teaspoon **Italian herb seasoning** (or ½ teaspoon *each* **oregano leaves** and **dry basil**). Spread over all sides of the **boneless center-cut leg of lamb** (2½ to 3 lb.). Roll up compactly; tie securely in several places. Place roast, fat side up, on a rack in a roasting pan. Insert a meat thermometer in thickest portion.

Roast, uncovered, in a 325° oven until meat thermometer registers 150° for medium rare (about 30 minutes per lb.). Remove to a serving platter.

Add ¾ cup **water** to pan drippings; scrape up browned bits from pan bottom and heat. Skim fat and pass juices at table to spoon over sliced lamb. Makes 4 to 6 servings.

Rack of Lamb for Two

 Preparation time: 5 minutes. Cooking time: 35 minutes

Picture an intimate dinner for two—starring a rack of lamb with four small chops for each of you. The size is perfect. Accompany with asparagus spears, broccoli, and shrimp-stuffed tomatoes (page 15). A scoop of vanilla ice cream with a little creme de menthe poured over makes a quick dessert.

1½ tablespoons butter or margarine, at room temperature
1 tablespoon minced parsley
1 small clove garlic, minced or pressed
Dash of salt and pepper
8-rib rack of lamb, Frenched (meat removed from ends of long chop bones)

Mix together butter, parsley, garlic, and salt and pepper until well blended. Rub mixture over lamb and place in a shallow roasting pan with rib bones pointing downward. Insert meat thermometer in thickest part of roast without touching bone.

Roast in a 425° oven for 35 minutes or until meat thermometer reaches 145° for medium-rare.

To serve, cut lamb between ribs. Four chops make 1 serving.

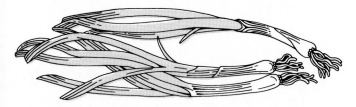

Miniature Moussaka

 Preparation time: 35 minutes. Cooking time: 20 minutes

A golden cheese layer tops a traditional eggplant moussaka. Assemble this ground lamb and eggplant casserole in a shallow baking dish or a medium-size (about 4½ by 8-inch) loaf pan.

1 small (¾ to 1 lb.) eggplant
About 3 tablespoons olive oil or salad oil
½ pound lean ground lamb or ground beef
½ cup chopped onion
1 clove garlic, minced or pressed
1 can (8 oz.) stewed tomatoes
1 can (2 oz.) mushroom stems and pieces
¼ cup catsup
¼ teaspoon *each* oregano leaves and ground cinnamon
2 tablespoons minced parsley
1 cup (about 4 oz.) shredded jack cheese
2 tablespoons grated Parmesan cheese

Rinse eggplant and pat dry; cut off and discard stem end and cut eggplant into ½-inch-thick slices. Brush eggplant slices liberally on both sides with oil; arrange in a single layer in a shallow pan. Bake in a 475° oven, turning if needed, until eggplant slices are well browned on both sides (about 30 minutes).

Meanwhile, in a wide frying pan over medium-high heat, cook ground meat until browned and crumbly. Add onion and garlic and cook for about 5 minutes until onion is limp. Discard any excess fat. Add tomatoes (break them up with a spoon), mushrooms and their liquid, catsup, oregano, cinnamon, and parsley. Cook, uncovered, over medium heat until sauce is thick (about 10 minutes).

Arrange ½ the eggplant in bottom of a shallow 1-quart baking dish, spoon over ½ the meat sauce, and sprinkle with ½ of the jack cheese. Repeat layers, using remaining eggplant, meat sauce, and jack cheese.

Sprinkle Parmesan cheese evenly over top. Bake, uncovered, in a 375° oven for about 20 minutes or until browned and bubbly.

Make-ahead Lamb Stew

Preparation time: 25 minutes. Cooking time: 1 hour and 35 minutes

To make this classic lamb stew ahead, cook it as directed, then refrigerate. Just before dinner time, reheat it slowly to serve with a crisp green salad and crusty French rolls. For dessert, serve wedges of honeydew melon with a squeeze of fresh lime.

1 pound lean boneless lamb stew meat, cut in 1-inch cubes
1½ tablespoons olive oil or salad oil
1 small clove garlic, minced or pressed
¾ cup regular-strength chicken broth
½ cup dry white wine (or additional chicken broth)
¼ teaspoon *each* rubbed sage and grated lemon peel
¼ teaspoon *each* marjoram and savory leaves
2 medium-size carrots
¼ pound small white boiling onions
3 small new potatoes (about 6 oz.), cut in ½-inch-thick slices
Chopped parsley

Trim excess fat and membrane from lamb. Heat oil in a wide frying pan over medium-high heat; add lamb and cook, uncovered, until well browned on all sides. Add garlic and cook, stirring, until lightly browned. Stir in chicken broth, wine, sage, lemon peel, marjoram, and savory. Cover and simmer for 1 hour.

Meanwhile, cut carrots diagonally in 1-inch lengths. Plunge onions into boiling water for about 1

minute; drain and peel. When lamb has simmered for 1 hour, add carrots, onions, and potato slices to the pan, then cover and simmer until vegetables are fork tender (about 35 minutes more).

With a slotted spoon, lift vegetables and meat from pan and place in individual bowls or deep plates. Turn heat to high and boil, uncovered, to reduce liquid to about ½ cup. Pour over stew. Sprinkle with parsley.

Sweet and Sour Stew

 Preparation time: 20 minutes. Cooking time: 1 hour and 55 minutes

A rich red sauce develops from the catsup-based sweet and sour mixture used as a cooking broth for lean beef or lamb stew meat. Serve with crusty French bread to soak up the juices. (See photograph on facing page.)

> 2 tablespoons all-purpose flour
> 1 teaspoon salt
> Dash of pepper
> 1 pound boneless, lean lamb stew meat or beef chuck, cut in 1-inch cubes
> 1½ tablespoons butter or margarine
> ¼ cup catsup
> 2 tablespoons *each* packed brown sugar and red wine vinegar
> 1½ teaspoons Worcestershire
> ½ cup water
> 6 small white boiling onions, peeled
> 2 large carrots, cut in 1-inch chunks
> Chopped parsley

Combine flour, ½ teaspoon of the salt, and pepper. Dredge meat pieces in flour mixture, shaking off excess.

In a deep 3 to 4-quart pan, melt butter over medium-high heat; add meat and brown well on all sides. Drain off and discard excess fat. Combine catsup, brown sugar, vinegar, Worcestershire, water, and remaining ½ teaspoon salt; add to meat. Add onions and simmer, covered, for 1 hour and 15 minutes, stirring once or twice. Add carrots and cook for about 40 minutes longer or until meat and vegetables are fork tender. Sprinkle with parsley.

SWEET AND SOUR STEW, richly laden with small onions and carrots, cooks unattended for several hours (recipe above). Serve this hearty dish with hunks of sourdough bread, garlic herb-flavored cheese, and radishes.

Oven-barbecued Country-style Spareribs

 Preparation time: 15 minutes. Cooking time: 2 hours

Plan on 2 hours for cooking thick, meaty spareribs topped first with lemon and onion, then with a well-seasoned sauce. Accompany the tangy ribs with crusty rolls and a butter lettuce salad.

> 1 to 1½ pounds country-style spareribs, trimmed of surface fat
> ½ lemon, thinly sliced
> 1 small onion, thinly sliced
> 2 tablespoons packed brown sugar
> 1 teaspoon chili powder
> ¼ teaspoon *each* celery seed and garlic salt
> ½ cup water
> ⅓ cup tomato-based chili sauce
> 2 tablespoons vinegar
> 1½ teaspoons *each* Worcestershire and soy sauce

Arrange spareribs in a single layer in an 8-inch-square baking dish. Distribute lemon and onion evenly over meat. Cover and bake in a 350° oven for 1 hour and 15 minutes.

Meanwhile, in a pan combine brown sugar, chili powder, celery seed, garlic salt, water, chili sauce, vinegar, Worcestershire, and soy sauce. Cook, uncovered, over medium heat for 5 minutes.

Remove lemon and onion slices and discard. Lift ribs from pan and cut in serving-size pieces. Discard pan drippings. Return meat to pan and pour hot sauce over. Continue baking, uncovered, basting frequently, for about 45 minutes or until meat is glazed and fork tender. Transfer meat to a serving dish. Skim off and discard any fat from sauce. Spoon sauce over meat.

Polish Sausage and Potatoes

 Preparation time (cooking included): 30 minutes

You use the same frying pan to cook each of the elements for this hearty entrée—start by browning the sausage, and while it cooks, prepare the vegetables and apple. Serve the sausage with mustard and horseradish, and a sliced tomato and cucumber salad with oil and vinegar dressing.

> About 6 tablespoons butter or margarine
> 8 to 10 ounces kielbasa
> 2 medium-size potatoes, peeled and thinly sliced
> 1 large onion, thinly sliced
> 1 large Golden Delicious apple

(Continued on next page)

Melt 1 tablespoon of the butter in a wide frying pan over medium heat. Slash sausage at 1-inch intervals and cook until browned on all sides. Arrange on a warm serving dish; keep warm.

Add 4 tablespoons of the butter to pan; add potatoes and onion and stir well. Cover and cook, turning often and adding more butter, if needed, until potatoes are tender (about 15 minutes).

Remove lid and continue cooking until potatoes are browned; arrange with sausage; keep warm.

Peel and core apple; cut into ½-inch-thick rings. Melt 1 more tablespoon butter in pan; add apple rings and cook until lightly browned on both sides. Arrange with sausage and potatoes.

Sweet and Sour Pork

🕐 *Preparation time (cooking included): 30 minutes*

A favorite among lovers of Chinese food, sweet and sour pork has endless variations. The one that follows is both quick and colorful. Have all the vegetables cut up and the sweet and sour sauce ready to go before you begin cooking.

    ¾ **pound lean boneless pork, cut in 1-inch cubes**
    1 **egg, beaten**
      About ¼ cup cornstarch
      About 2½ tablespoons salad oil
    1 **small onion, cut in 1-inch squares**
    1 **medium-size carrot, sliced diagonally ¼ inch thick**
    1 **small clove garlic, minced or pressed**
    1 **small green pepper, seeded and cut in 1-inch squares**
    1 **can (8¼ oz.) sliced pineapple, drained and cut in pieces, or ¾ cup fresh pineapple chunks**
    1 **medium-size tomato, cut in 1-inch cubes**
      Sweet and sour sauce (recipe follows)

Dip pork pieces in egg, drain briefly, and roll in cornstarch until lightly coated on all sides; shake off excess. Heat 1½ tablespoons of the oil in a wide frying pan over medium-high heat. Add pork and cook, turning constantly with a wide spatula, until browned (about 7 minutes). Lift pork from pan and set aside; scrape free and discard any browned particles, leaving oil in pan.

Add enough oil to pan to make about 1 tablespoon total. Place over highest heat. Add onion, carrot, and garlic; cook, stirring, for about 3 minutes or until vegetables are tender-crisp. Add green pepper, pineapple, tomato, and sweet and sour sauce; cook, stirring, over high heat until mixture boils. Add pork, then cook and stir for 1 minute longer to heat through and coat pork with sauce.

Sweet and sour sauce. Stir together 1½ teaspoons **cornstarch** and 2½ tablespoons packed **brown sugar.** Stir in ¼ teaspoon grated **fresh ginger root** or ⅛ teaspoon ground ginger, 1½ teaspoons *each* **soy sauce** and **dry sherry,** and 2 tablespoons *each* **wine vinegar** and **water.**

Pork Tenderloin with Onion-Apple Cream

🕐 *Preparation time: 20 minutes. Cooking time: 25 minutes*

Baste a small whole pork tenderloin with sherry-flavored cream as it roasts. The same basting sauce flavors slow-cooked apples and onions. Serve green beans and warm, soft rolls alongside.

    1 **whole pork tenderloin (about 12 oz.)**
      Sherry baste (recipe follows)
    1 **large onion, thinly sliced**
    1 **small Golden Delicious apple, thinly sliced**
    2 **tablespoons butter or margarine**
      Parsley sprigs

Place pork tenderloin on rack in a broiler pan; insert meat thermometer into thickest part. Brush pork with sherry baste. Cook in a 425° oven for 25 to 30 minutes or until meat thermometer registers 170°; baste frequently during roasting.

Meanwhile, melt butter in a wide frying pan over medium heat. Add onion and apple and cook, stirring frequently, until limp and golden (about 20 minutes). Add remaining sherry baste and bring to a boil; place in a small serving bowl. Garnish meat with parsley sprigs and pass onion-apple cream to spoon over.

Sherry baste. Mix together 6 tablespoons **whipping cream,** 2 tablespoons **cream sherry,** 1 teaspoon **Dijon mustard,** and ½ teaspoon *each* **salt** and prepared **horseradish.**

Mushroom-topped Pork Chops

⏱ *Preparation time: 10 minutes. Cooking time: 30 minutes*

Add fresh mushrooms to mushroom soup and you have a supereasy, mellow sauce for pan-fried pork chops.

4 center cut loin pork chops, cut 1 inch thick
   Pepper
½ pound mushrooms, sliced
1 can (10½ oz.) condensed cream of mushroom soup

Trim fat from chops; add a piece of fat to a wide frying pan. Cook over medium heat until pan is well greased; discard fat. Add pork chops, sprinkle with pepper, and cook over medium heat until browned on both sides; remove from pan. Add mushrooms to pan and cook, stirring, until lightly browned and liquid has evaporated; stir in soup. Arrange chops in sauce. Cook, covered, over low heat for about 30 minutes or until meat is fork tender.

Pork Chops with Rhubarb Dressing

⏱ *Preparation time: 15 minutes. Cooking time: 1 hour*

Rhubarb cooks down to make a sweet-sour sauce for both chops and dressing. Complete the meal with fresh buttered peas, and ice cream for dessert.

⅛ teaspoon dry rosemary, crumbled
½ teaspoon salt
   Dash pepper
2 pork loin or shoulder chops, cut ¾ inch thick
1 tablespoon salad oil
2 slices firm-textured bread, cut into ½-inch cubes (about 1¾ cups)
⅓ cup firmly packed brown sugar
¼ teaspoon ground cinnamon
⅛ teaspoon ground allspice
1 pound rhubarb, cut into ½-inch pieces (about 3 cups)
1½ tablespoons all-purpose flour

Mix together rosemary, salt, and pepper. Sprinkle evenly over chops. Heat oil in a wide frying pan over medium-high heat; add chops and brown on both sides; set aside with drippings.

Stir together bread cubes, brown sugar, cinnamon, allspice, rhubarb, and flour; spread half the mixture in a greased shallow 1½ to 2-quart baking dish. Arrange chops on top; spoon over 2 tablespoons drippings (add water if necessary, to make this amount); top with remaining rhubarb mixture. Cover and refrigerate if made ahead. Bake, covered, in a 350° oven for 45 minutes; then uncover and bake for 15 minutes longer or until pork is fork tender.

Linguisa and Garbanzo Stew

⏱ *Preparation time: 15 minutes. Cooking time: 30 minutes*

Unlike some stews, this one needs only a half-hour of simmering to be ready for the table. Canned garbanzos contribute to the speed, and sausage lends its piquant flavor.

1 tablespoon olive oil or salad oil
1 small onion, chopped
2 cups shredded cabbage
1 can (about 1 lb.) garbanzos
   About ½ pound linguisa or Polish sausage
1 hard-cooked egg, thinly sliced or pressed through a sieve
   Pitted ripe olives

Heat oil in a wide frying pan over medium heat; add onion and cabbage and cook, stirring, until vegetables are limp and lightly browned. Stir in garbanzos and their liquid. Cut linguisa into 2-inch chunks and add to pan. Cover and simmer for 30 minutes, stirring occasionally. Skim and discard fat. Ladle into soup plates and garnish with hard-cooked egg and olives.

POULTRY

From the simplest oven-fried chicken thighs to the grandest Cornish hens—plump and somehow complete in miniature, under a flaming cherry sauce—poultry appears to have been designed expressly to accommodate the for-two cook. As if the availability of small birds weren't enough of a boon, it's a simple matter in most markets to buy only the pieces you need and like best; and nowadays that's true not just of chicken but even of turkey, once the province of only the most patient eaters of leftovers.

In this chapter you'll find recipes for cooking chicken with fruits, vegetables, nuts, surprising seasonings, fragrant sauces. Cornish hens appear in two versions, turkey meat in three.

The amounts of poultry you'll buy will depend on your appetite and on what other ingredients are going into the meal. Quantities specified in our recipes reflect the latter variable, and with a little experimenting you'll solve the former.

General rules are that a 2 to 2½-pound broiler-fryer is ample for two; a large whole chicken breast serves two, though you may prefer to offer one small breast apiece. Two small Cornish hens serve two generously; a single large one would also serve two. A duck—with high fat content that makes it unique among birds—will lose much fat as it cooks, so that a 4 to 5-pound duckling will yield only 2 to 3 servings.

Crusty Oven-fried Chicken

Preparation time: 15 minutes. Cooking time: 1 hour

Soy-marinated chicken is coated with seasoned crumbs and sesame seed, then baked to crispy doneness in the oven (See photograph on facing page.)

- ¼ cup soy sauce
- 1 tablespoon salad oil
- 1 small clove garlic, minced or pressed
- 2 to 4 chicken legs with thighs attached (about ½ lb. *each*)
- ¼ cup wheat germ
- 2 tablespoons fine dry bread crumbs
- 1 tablespoon *each* sesame seed and chopped parsley
- ¼ teaspoon *each* pepper and paprika
  Parsley (optional)

Combine soy sauce, oil, and garlic. Arrange chicken in a single layer in a shallow baking dish. Pour soy mixture over chicken, turn chicken to coat all sides, and let stand for about 10 minutes.

Meanwhile, mix together wheat germ, bread crumbs, sesame seed, chopped parsley, pepper, and paprika.

Lift chicken from marinade, drain, then turn over in wheat germ mixture to evenly coat all sides; shake off excess. Arrange coated chicken on a well-greased rimmed baking sheet. Bake, uncovered, in a 350° oven for about 1 hour or until thigh meat near bone is no longer pink when slashed. Remove to serving platter and garnish with parsley, if desired.

Curried Chicken

Preparation time: 10 minutes. Cooking time: 35 minutes

Each of you gets a chicken half, butter-broiled to succulency. Broiling eliminates messy pan-frying and the cleanup that follows.

- 2 tablespoons butter or margarine, at room temperature
- 1 tablespoon curry powder
- ¼ teaspoon *each* ground ginger and ground cloves
  Dash *each* salt and pepper
- 2 to 2½ pound broiler-fryer chicken, split in half
- ½ cup dry white wine, dry vermouth, or regular-strength chicken broth

(Continued on next page)

FINGER-FOOD DINNER features sesame seed coated oven-fried chicken (recipe above), French fried potatoes, and whole fresh fruit.

In a small bowl, combine butter, curry powder, ginger, cloves, salt, and pepper. With a sharp knife, cut several small slits in skin of chicken over breasts and thighs. Push about ¾ of the butter mixture in between skin and flesh.

Melt remaining butter mixture and stir in white wine. Place chicken halves, skin side down, on rack in broiler pan. Broil 6 to 8 inches below heat for 20 minutes, basting several times with wine mixture. Turn chicken pieces over and continue broiling and basting for 15 to 20 minutes or until meat is no longer pink when slashed in thickest part.

Transfer chicken to serving platter. Skim and discard fat from pan juices, then pour juices over chicken.

Chicken Sauté with Green Beans

Preparation time: 10 minutes. Cooking time: 50 minutes

Chicken sautéed with green beans makes its own sauce, simmering in cream and wine. Serve it with parsley-buttered potatoes and vegetable relishes.

½ teaspooon salt
Dash pepper
2 tablespoons all-purpose flour
2 to 2½-pound broiler-fryer, cut in quarters
1½ tablespoons butter or margarine
¼ pound mushrooms, sliced
1 tablespoon freeze-dried shallots
⅓ cup *each* whipping cream and dry white wine
1 cup frozen cut green beans, thawed
Walnut halves (optional)

Mix together salt, pepper, and flour. Dredge chicken in mixture to coat; shake off excess. In a wide frying pan over medium heat, melt butter; add chicken and brown well on all sides, adding more butter, if needed (about 15 minutes). Stir in mushrooms, shallots, cream, and wine. Cover and simmer for 25 minutes. Add beans, cover, and simmer for 10 to 15 minutes or just until meat is no longer pink when slashed in thickest part. Remove chicken and vegetables to a serving dish. Boil cooking liquid, uncovered, until slightly thickened. Pour sauce over chicken and vegetables. Garnish with walnuts, if you wish.

Chicken sauté for one. Use 1 quarter of a 3 to 3½-pound **chicken.** Sprinkle with **salt** and **pepper** to taste and enough all-purpose **flour** to coat lightly. Cook in 1 tablespoon **butter,** adding 3 sliced **mushrooms,** 2 teaspoons chopped **shallots,** ¼ cup *each* **whipping cream** and dry **white wine,** and ½ cup frozen cut **green beans.**

Simple Pâté

When you want a little appetizer before dinner, think of this chicken liver pâté. Save the livers from just two chickens (they freeze well). Serve pâté on Melba toast.

In a frying pan over medium-low heat, cook 2 **chicken livers** in 1 tablespoon **butter** or margarine until just pink in center when slashed (about 5 minutes). In a blender or food processor, chop livers with butter and ⅓ of a small package (3-oz. size) **cream cheese,** a few drops **liquid hot pepper seasoning,** ¼ teaspoon **salt,** 1 tablespoon chopped **green pepper,** and 1 teaspoon **dry sherry.** Cover and chill. Serve with **Melba toast** or crisp rye crackers. Makes ⅓ cup.

Chicken with Artichokes

Preparation time: 15 minutes. Cooking time: 20-40 minutes

An attractive chicken dish is this one baked with artichoke hearts and sliced mushrooms and flavored with sherry. Serve with rice, if you wish.

2 whole chicken breasts (about ¾ lb. *each*), split, or 2 *each* legs and thighs
Salt, pepper, and paprika
About 1 tablespoon *each* butter or margarine and salad oil
1 package (about 9 oz.) frozen artichoke hearts, thawed
5 medium-size mushrooms, sliced
4 teaspoons all-purpose flour
½ cup water
2 tablespoons dry sherry
1 teaspoon chicken stock base
⅛ teaspoon dry rosemary, crumbled
Minced parsley

Sprinkle chicken lightly with salt, pepper, and paprika. In a wide frying pan, cook chicken in butter and oil over medium-high heat until browned. Arrange chicken in a 1 to 1½-quart casserole with artichoke hearts.

Cook mushrooms in pan drippings until liquid evaporates; sprinkle mushrooms with flour and stir to blend. Gradually stir in water, sherry, chicken stock base, and rosemary. Cook, stirring, until slightly thickened; pour over chicken. Cover and bake in a 375° oven for 20 minutes for breasts (40 minutes for legs) or until meat is no longer pink when slashed in thickest part. Garnish with minced parsley.

Chicken with Sweet Onions

 Preparation time: 20 minutes. Cooking time: 25 to 45 minutes

Generously topped with flavorful onions and toasted almonds, your choice of meaty chicken pieces—dark or light—will make a beautiful, easy baked dish.

 3 tablespoons slivered almonds
 ½ teaspoon salt
   Dash *each* pepper and paprika
   About 1½ pounds meaty chicken pieces
 2 tablespoons butter or margarine
 2 large onions, thinly sliced
 1 tablespoon packed brown sugar
 ¼ teaspoon ground cinnamon
   Lemon wedges

Spread almonds in a shallow pan and toast in a 350° oven for 8 to 10 minutes or until golden; set aside.

Mix together salt, pepper, and paprika; sprinkle evenly over chicken. Arrange chicken, skin side down, in a shallow greased 2-quart baking dish. Bake, uncovered, in a 400° oven 30 minutes for dark meat, 15 minutes for white meat. Turn meat over and bake 15 minutes for dark meat, 10 minutes for white meat or until no longer pink when slashed in thickest part.

Meanwhile, melt butter in wide frying pan over medium-low heat. Add onion, separating into rings, and cook slowly, uncovered, stirring often, until onion is limp and golden (about 30 minutes); onion should not show signs of browning during first 15 minutes—if it does, reduce heat. Sprinkle with brown sugar and cinnamon; stir to blend.

Cover chicken with onion mixture, sprinkle with toasted almonds, and serve with lemon wedges to squeeze over servings.

Chicken Cacciatore

 Preparation time: 15 minutes. Cooking time: 50 minutes

This familiar Italian dish cooks in less than an hour, yet achieves a traditionally robust flavor. The chicken and sauce are good with green noodles.

 1 tablespoon butter or margarine
 1 tablespoon olive oil
 2 whole chicken legs with thighs attached (about ½ lb. *each*)
 ¼ pound mushrooms, sliced
 1 small onion, sliced
 1 green pepper, seeded and finely chopped
 1 clove garlic, minced or pressed
 ¼ cup dry white wine or regular-strength chicken broth
 1 can (8 oz.) tomato sauce
 ¾ teaspoon salt
 ⅛ teaspoon *each* marjoram, oregano, and thyme leaves, crumbled
 ½ teaspoon chicken stock base
 1 tablespoon minced parsley

Heat butter and oil in a wide frying pan over medium-high heat. Add chicken and cook, turning, until browned on all sides; remove from pan and set aside. Add mushrooms, onion, green pepper, and garlic to pan drippings and cook, stirring, until onion is limp (about 5 minutes). Stir in wine, tomato sauce, salt, marjoram, oregano, thyme, stock base, and parsley.

Return chicken to pan. Bring liquid to boiling, reduce heat, cover, and simmer for about 40 minutes or until meat is no longer pink when slashed in thickest part. If sauce is too thin, remove chicken to a serving dish and keep warm; bring sauce to a boil, then cook, uncovered, stirring, until slightly thickened. Pour over chicken.

Chicken with New Potatoes and Carrots

 Preparation time: 10 minutes. Cooking time: 50 minutes

Everything for dinner bakes together in the oven. You can even bake dessert—frozen fruit turnovers to serve flaky and hot with ice cream—at the same time.

 2 tablespoons *each* fine dry bread crumbs and yellow cornmeal
 ¾ teaspoon curry powder
 ⅛ teaspoon salt
   Dash pepper
 2 to 2½-pound broiler-fryer chicken, cut in quarters
 ¼ cup butter or margarine
 4 small carrots, peeled
 4 small whole new potatoes (*each* about 1½ inches in diameter)
   Chopped parsley

(Continued on next page)

In a small bag combine crumbs, cornmeal, curry powder, salt, and pepper. Shake chicken quarters, 1 at a time, in bag to coat completely; set aside. In a 9 by 13-inch baking dish, melt butter in oven while it is preheating to 400°. Tilt pan slightly so butter collects in one corner; roll carrots and potatoes in butter to coat evenly, then push to one side. Coat chicken with butter, laying pieces skin side down beside vegetables.

Bake, uncovered, in a 400° oven for 30 minutes. Turn vegetables and chicken over and bake for 20 minutes longer or until vegetables are fork tender and chicken is no longer pink when slashed in thickest part. Sprinkle with parsley.

Chicken Breasts Veronique

 Preparation time: 15 minutes. Cooking time: 25 minutes

For a special occasion, serve this elegant dish that's highlighted by a delicate cream sauce and seedless green grapes; sautéed whole mushrooms are the garnish. Just add a butter lettuce salad. (See photograph on facing page.)

    2 whole chicken breasts (about ¾ lb. *each*), split, boned, and skinned
       Salt
    3 tablespoons butter or margarine
    1 tablespoon orange marmalade
    ¼ teaspoon tarragon, crumbled
    ¼ cup dry white wine
    8 medium-size mushrooms, fluted, and stems trimmed
    ¼ cup whipping cream
    ¾ cup seedless grapes
       Parsley sprigs

Sprinkle chicken lightly with salt. Melt 1 tablespoon of the butter in wide frying pan over medium heat. Add chicken breasts and cook until golden on each side. Stir in marmalade, tarragon, and wine. Cover and simmer for about 15 minutes or until meat is no longer pink when slashed in thickest part. Transfer to warm serving dish.

Meanwhile, melt remaining 2 tablespoons butter in a small pan, over medium heat. Add mushrooms and cook, stirring, until liquid evaporates.

To pan juices add cream and quickly bring to a full rolling boil. Mix in grapes, return to a boil, then pour sauce over chicken. Garnish with sautéed mushrooms and parsley sprigs.

Chicken breast veronique for one. Use 1 whole **chicken breast,** 2 teaspoons *each* **butter** or margarine and

marmalade, ⅛ teaspoon **tarragon,** 2 tablespoons *each* dry **white wine** and **whipping cream,** and ⅓ cup **seedless grapes.** Cook 4 whole **mushrooms** in 1 tablespoon **butter** or margarine.

Chicken Scallopini

 Preparation time: 10 minutes. Cooking time: 7 minutes

Boned chicken breasts are a versatile ingredient, ideal for a quick but special dinner for two. Try them pounded and cooked as scallopini with either a brandy cream sauce or a lemon mustard sauce. Both are delicious with broccoli or asparagus spears.

    2 whole chicken breasts (about ¾ lb. *each*), split, boned, and skinned
    2 to 3 tablespoons butter or margarine
       Salt and pepper
    2 tablespoons brandy
    ¼ cup whipping cream

Place chicken breasts, cut side down, about 5 to 6 inches apart between 2 sheets of clear plastic wrap or wax paper. Pound with smooth side of a mallet until pieces are no more than ⅛ inch thick.

In a wide frying pan, melt 2 tablespoons of the butter over medium-high heat. Add chicken breasts and cook, uncovered, until lightly browned on each side, adding more butter if needed to prevent sticking. Sprinkle chicken with salt and pepper.

Warm brandy in a small container, pour over chicken, and at once set aflame *(not under an exhaust fan or flammable items)*; shake pan until flame dies.

Remove from heat and with a slotted spoon quickly lift chicken from juices to a serving dish; keep warm. Return frying pan to highest heat and add cream. Boil rapidly, uncovered, scraping up browned particles, until large shiny bubbles form. Drain any accumulated juices from chicken into sauce, then spoon over chicken and serve.

Chicken with lemon mustard sauce. Follow recipe for chicken scallopini (preceding), making these changes: Instead of brandy, use 2 tablespoons **lemon juice;** omit flaming. Add 2 teaspoons **Dijon mustard** with **whipping cream.**

(Continued on page 52)

FOR AN ELEGANT DINNER, an elegant entrée—Chicken Breasts Véronique (recipe at left). A delicate cream sauce coats boned chicken breasts, fluted mushrooms, and green grapes. Serve with butter lettuce tossed with vinaigrette (page 15).

Chicken with lemon mustard sauce for one. Use 1 whole chicken breast, split; brown it in about 1 tablespoon **butter** or margarine. Use 1 tablespoon **lemon juice,** 2 to 3 tablespoons **whipping cream,** and 1 teaspoon **Dijon mustard.**

Slivered Chicken and Walnuts

 Preparation time (cooking included): 10 minutes

Dinner is on the table in minutes when you stir-fry. Assemble chicken, nuts, ginger, and seasoning sauce; then cook and eat.

    Cooking sauce (recipe follows)
1 **whole chicken breast (about 1 lb.), boned and skinned**
1 **tablespoon soy sauce**
1 **teaspoon cornstarch**
3 **tablespoons salad oil**
½ **cup walnut halves**
1 **medium-size green pepper, seeded and cut into 1-inch squares**
½ **teaspoon finely minced fresh ginger or ¼ teaspoon ground ginger**

Prepare cooking sauce; set aside. Cut chicken into thin strips; mix with soy and cornstarch and set aside.

Heat oil over medium-high heat in a wok or wide frying pan; add nuts and cook, stirring, until brown; remove with slotted spoon. Add chicken to oil; cook, stirring, until opaque (about 1½ minutes); lift out. Add pepper and ginger; cook, stirring, until pepper is bright green. Add chicken and cooking sauce; cook, stirring, until thick (about 1 minute); add nuts and serve.

Cooking sauce. Thoroughly blend ½ teaspoon **cornstarch,** dash **liquid hot pepper seasoning,** ¾ teaspoon *each* **sugar** and **wine vinegar,** 1 teaspoon **dry sherry** or water, and 1 tablespoon **soy sauce.**

Spicy Barbecued Chicken

 Preparation time: 10 minutes. Marinating time: 4 hours. Heat coals: 35 minutes. Cooking time: 40 minutes

In the morning or the night before, start the chicken legs marinating in a spicy Pakistani-style yogurt mixture for barbecuing in the evening. Serve them with cool tomato-cucumber sauce—this, too, can be made ahead. Add a butter lettuce salad and fresh fruit.

2 **whole chicken legs with thighs attached (about ½ lb. *each*)**
⅓ **cup unflavored yogurt**
¼ **teaspoon ground ginger**
½ **teaspoon *each* salt and garlic powder**
⅛ **teaspoon cayenne**
1 **tablespoon lemon juice**
    Lemon wedges
    Tomato-cucumber sauce (recipe follows)

Remove chicken skin, if you wish. Slash each piece of chicken 2 or 3 times about halfway to the bone; place in a shallow, close-fitting pan. Combine yogurt, ginger, salt, garlic powder, cayenne, and lemon juice; pour over chicken, cover, and refrigerate for 4 to 6 hours or until next day, turning occasionally, if possible.

Lift chicken from marinade, drain briefly, and place on a barbecue grill about 6 inches above a solid bed of low-glowing coals. Cook, turning and lightly brushing with marinade, until meat is well browned on all sides and no longer pink when slashed in thickest part (40 to 50 minutes). Serve with lemon wedges and tomato-cucumber sauce to spoon over.

Tomato-cucumber sauce. Stir together ½ cup **unflavored yogurt;** 1 small **tomato,** peeled and finely diced; ½ cup finely diced, peeled **cucumber;** 2 thinly sliced **green onions** (including some green tops); ½ teaspoon ground **cumin;** ¼ teaspoon **salt;** and 1 tablespoon finely chopped fresh **coriander** (cilantro— or use 1 teaspoon dried cilantro), watercress, or mint. Cover and chill thoroughly. Makes about ¾ cup.

reduce heat, and simmer until chicken is no longer pink when slashed in thickest part (12 to 15 minutes). Remove chicken from pan with a slotted spoon; keep warm.

Add peas, asparagus (if used), and cream to pan. Bring to a boil over high heat; boil, stirring often, until sauce is slightly thickened (about 3 minutes). Spoon over chicken and serve at once.

Garlic Chicken and New Potatoes

Preparation time: 10 minutes. Cooking time: 45 minutes

Slow cooking transforms the pungency of garlic to a surprising sweetness.

- 2 **tablespoons olive oil or salad oil**
- 2 **chicken legs with thighs attached (about ½ lb. *each*)**
- 4 **small new potatoes (about 2 inches in diameter) or 2 medium-size potatoes (about 4 inches in diameter), cut in half**
- ½ **teaspoon dry rosemary**
- 2 **tablespoons water**
- 12 **cloves garlic, slightly crushed**
  Salt and pepper

Heat oil in a wide frying pan over medium-high heat and add chicken and potatoes. Cook, turning potatoes occasionally and chicken once, until chicken is browned on both sides (about 15 minutes).

Reduce heat to low and add rosemary and water; cover and cook for 15 minutes. Turn chicken and potatoes over and add garlic. Cover and cook, turning potatoes and garlic occasionally, until meat is no longer pink when slashed in thickest part (about 15 minutes). Add salt and pepper to taste.

Chicken Liver Sauté

Preparation time: 5 minutes. Cooking time: 7 minutes

For a brunch or quick supper, serve chicken liver sauté over toasted English muffins.

- 2 **to 3 tablespoons butter or margarine**
- ¾ **pound chicken livers, halved**
- ¼ **pound mushrooms, quartered**
- 1½ **teaspoons all-purpose flour**
- ¼ **teaspoon *each* fines herbes and salt**
- 2 **tablespoons dry sherry**
- ¼ **cup regular-strength chicken broth**
- 2 **English muffins, split and buttered**
  Chopped parsley

(Continued on page 55)

Chicken Primavera

Preparation time: 20 minutes.
Cooking time: 25 to 30 minutes

Serve this colorful chicken over fresh tagliarini or fettuccine. (See cover photograph.)

- 1 **large or 2 small whole chicken breasts (about 1½ lb. total), split, boned, and skinned**
  Salt, white pepper, and all-purpose flour
- 2 **tablespoons butter or margarine**
- ¼ **pound mushrooms, sliced**
- 2 **shallots, finely chopped (about ¼ cup)**
- ¼ **teaspoon dry tarragon**
- ⅛ **teaspoon ground nutmeg**
- 2 **ounces thinly sliced prosciutto, cut in ½-inch-wide strips**
- 1 **medium-size carrot, cut in 3-inch-long julienne strips**
- ½ **cup dry white wine**
- ¼ **cup frozen tiny peas**
- 3 **asparagus spears, cut in ½-inch-thick slanting slices (optional)**
- ½ **cup whipping cream**

Sprinkle chicken on all sides with salt and pepper; dust with flour. Melt butter in a wide frying pan over medium-high heat. Add chicken and cook, turning as needed, until golden on all sides; remove from pan.

Add mushrooms to pan and cook until lightly browned (about 5 minutes); stir in shallots. Return chicken to pan. Sprinkle with tarragon, nutmeg, and prosciutto; add carrot strips around chicken. Pour in wine. Cover,

Melt 2 tablespoons of the butter in a wide frying pan over medium-high heat. Add livers and mushrooms and cook just until livers are browned, adding more butter if needed. Stir in flour, fines herbes, and salt; remove from heat and gradually stir in sherry and chicken broth. Return to heat and cook, stirring, for about 3 minutes or until thickened.

Meanwhile, toast muffins in a toaster oven or broiler. Serve chicken livers over muffins; sprinkle with parsley.

Game Hens with Flaming Cherry Sauce

🕐 *Thaw frozen birds. Preparation time: 10 minutes. Cooking time: 1 hour*

Flaming a dish at the table is dramatic enough for the most special occasion, easy enough for everyday. And Cornish hens make any dinner seem festive. (See photograph on facing page.)

> 2 **Rock Cornish game hens (16 to 20 oz. e*ach*)**
> **Seasoned salt and pepper**
> 2 **tablespoons butter or margarine, melted**
> ½ **teaspoon e*ach* seasoned salt, ground ginger, and paprika**
> **Cherry sauce (recipe follows)**
> **Orange slices**
> 2 **tablespoons brandy (optional)**

Thaw hens as directed on package (set giblets aside for other uses); rinse hens and pat dry. Sprinkle inside cavities with seasoned salt and pepper. Place hens slightly apart, breast sides up, in a roasting pan.

Combine butter with the ½ teaspoon seasoned salt, ginger, and paprika; brush over hens, using it all. Bake hens, uncovered, in a 350° oven for about 1 hour or until leg joints move easily; during last half hour, baste birds several times with pan drippings. Meanwhile, prepare cherry sauce; keep warm over low heat or in a chafing dish.

When hens are roasted, discard excess fat from pan juices and stir juices into cherry sauce. Arrange hens on serving plates and garnish with orange slices; keep warm. To flame birds, warm brandy in a small container; ignite (not under an exhaust fan or flammable items) and pour, flaming, into sauce. While still flaming, spoon sauce over birds.

FOR A DRAMATIC ENTRÉE, flame Cornish game hens with brandied cherry sauce at the table just before serving (recipe above). Allow one hen per hungry diner and let orange slices and broccoli spears round out the menu.

Cherry sauce. Drain 1 small can (about 8 oz.) pitted **dark sweet cherries,** reserving ⅓ cup syrup. In a pan, combine reserved syrup with ⅔ cup **water,** 1 **chicken bouillon cube,** 1 small **onion** (cut in wedges), 8 whole **cloves,** and ¼ teaspoon ground **cinnamon.** Bring to a boil, stirring; then reduce heat and simmer, uncovered, for 10 minutes; strain, discarding cloves and onion.

Return sauce to pan. Stir together 1 tablespoon *each* **cornstarch** and **water** until smooth; stir into sauce and cook, stirring, until it boils and thickens. Stir in cherries, ¼ teaspoon **grated lemon peel,** and 1 tablespoon **lemon juice.**

Game Hens with Papaya and Curry Pilaf

🕐 *Thaw frozen birds. Preparation time: 15 minutes. Cooking time: 1 hour*

Curried pilaf bakes alongside the chutney basted game hens. Garnish the hens with papaya slices heated briefly in the game hen juices.

> 2 **Rock Cornish game hens (16 to 20 oz. e*ach*)**
> **Salt and pepper**
> 2 **tablespoons butter or margarine, melted**
> 1 **teaspoon curry powder**
> **Curry pilaf (recipe follows)**
> 3 **tablespoons Major Grey's chutney, finely chopped**
> 2 **tablespoons lime juice**
> 1 **large (or 2 small) papaya**
> **Lime wedges**

Thaw hens as directed on package (set giblets aside for other uses); rinse hens and pat dry. Sprinkle inside cavities with salt and pepper. Place hens slightly apart, breast sides up, in a roasting pan. Combine butter and curry; brush over hens, using it all. Roast, uncovered, in a 350° oven for about 1 hour or until leg joints move easily. Meanwhile, prepare pilaf and set into oven alongside hens.

After 30 minutes' roasting, remove hens from oven, stir chutney and lime juice into pan drippings, and baste hens with mixture. Return to oven and continue baking, basting hens with drippings 2 or 3 times.

Remove hens from pan and arrange on a warm serving plate; keep warm. Peel papaya, cut in half, and discard seeds. Cut in ½-inch-thick slices. Turn papaya in pan drippings, then return to oven until papaya is heated through (about 5 minutes). Remove papaya from oven and arrange around hens; spoon pan juices over top. Garnish with lime wedges and serve with curry pilaf.

(Continued on next page)

Curry pilaf. In a wide frying pan over medium heat, melt 2 tablespoons **butter** or margarine. Stir in 1 small **onion,** chopped; 1 clove **garlic,** minced or pressed; and 1 teaspoon **curry powder.** Cook, stirring, over medium heat, for about 2 minutes. Add 1 cup **long-grain rice;** cook, stirring, for about 5 minutes. Add 2¼ cups **regular-strength chicken broth** (or 3 chicken bouillon cubes mixed with 2¼ cups water) and ½ teaspoon **salt.** Transfer to a 1½ to 2-quart baking dish. Cover and bake in a 350° oven for 30 to 45 minutes or until rice is tender to bite and liquid is absorbed.

Turkey Schnitzel

 Preparation time: 10 minutes. Marinating time: 30 minutes. Cooking time: 6 minutes

Some markets slice and package uncooked turkey breast meat so that it can be purchased easily in amounts just right for two. Or you can purchase a half or whole breast, slice the meat for this recipe, then roast or poach the remainder to use in sandwiches, salads, and casseroles.

- **4 turkey breast slices, cut about ½ inch thick (about ¾ lb. total)**
- **2 tablespoons lemon juice**
- **¼ cup olive oil or salad oil**
- **⅛ teaspoon *each* salt and pepper**
- **⅓ cup *each* all-purpose flour and grated Parmesan cheese**
- **2 to 3 tablespoons butter or margarine**

Place meat between 2 sheets of wax paper or plastic wrap and pound ¼ inch thick with smooth side of a mallet. Mix together lemon juice, oil, salt, and pepper. Place pounded turkey in a shallow pan and pour over lemon juice mixture; cover and refrigerate at least 30 minutes or as long as overnight.

Drain liquid from turkey. Mix together flour and Parmesan cheese; coat turkey generously with mixture and shake off excess. Heat 2 tablespoons of the butter in a wide frying pan over medium-high heat. Quickly cook turkey slices until lightly browned on both sides (3 to 5 minutes per side), adding more butter if needed.

Braised Turkey Drumsticks

 Preparation time: 10 minutes. Cooking time: 2 hours and 15 minutes

Cooked to moist tenderness in a wine and broth mixture with celery and carrots, these turkey legs are good with baked potatoes and mixed sweet pickles. You'll want to make this dish when you have a little time—it takes about 2 hours to cook.

- **2 tablespoons butter or margarine**
- **2 small turkey legs (1½ to 1¾ lb. total)**
- **1 small clove garlic, minced or pressed**
- **1 medium-size onion, sliced and separated into rings**
- **1 large stalk celery, thinly sliced diagonally**
- **2 medium-size carrots, thinly sliced diagonally**
- **¼ cup *each* regular-strength chicken broth and dry white wine (or ½ cup broth)**
- **½ teaspoon seasoned salt**
  Dash pepper
  Chopped parsley

Melt butter in a wide frying pan over medium-high heat. Add turkey and cook until browned on all sides. Add garlic, onion, celery, and carrots; cook until onion is limp. Stir in chicken broth, wine, seasoned salt, and pepper. Bring to a boil, reduce heat, cover tightly, and simmer 2 hours or until turkey is very tender when pierced.

With a slotted spoon, remove turkey and vegetables to a warm serving dish. Over high heat, boil pan juices to reduce by about ⅓; pour over turkey. Sprinkle with parsley.

Turkey and Fried Rice

Cook rice ahead. Preparation time: 10 minutes. Cooking time: 10 minutes

When you have cooked turkey at hand, this dish can be put together quickly. With a green salad, it makes a satisfying supper. Plan to cook the rice in advance.

- **2 tablespoons salad oil**
- **¼ cup *each* chopped onion and green bell pepper**
- **1 cup cold cooked rice**
- **1 clove garlic, minced or pressed**
  About 1½ cups thinly sliced celery, carrots, mushrooms, water chestnuts, or zucchini
- **1½ cups cooked turkey cut in bite-size pieces**
- **1 egg, beaten**
- **1 tablespoon soy sauce**
- **4 cherry tomatoes, quartered**
  Chopped green onion or parsley

Heat oil in a wide frying pan or wok over medium-high heat; add onion and pepper and cook, stirring, until onion is limp. Sprinkle in rice and garlic and stir constantly until rice is evenly coated with oil. Add vegetables and cook, stirring, for 2 to 4 minutes (vegetables should be tender crisp). Stir in meat to heat throughly, then push mixture to sides of pan. Pour in egg and cook until just set; add soy and tomatoes and mix into rice along with egg. Turn into a serving dish. Sprinkle with green onion or parsley.

SEAFOOD

Seafood has all kinds of advantages. High in nutrition, it is low in calories and fat. It has little waste and is easily purchased in quantities just right for one or two. It cooks quickly—indeed, you should be careful not to overcook, and a good rule with fish is to allow 10 minutes cooking time per inch of thickness.

But seafood's greatest attribute is its wonderful taste, followed closely by its versatility. In this chapter are recipes for fish blanketed in delicate sauces, stir-fried teriyaki-style, sautéed with butter and almonds, baked in casseroles, simmered in stews. All are surprisingly quick to prepare and marvelous to eat.

Our recipes give quantities, but to guide you in general buying of seafood, we offer the following:

When you buy boneless fillets or steaks, allow ¾ to 1 pound for two people; small whole fish such as trout, about 1½ pounds. For shrimp in the shell, about a pound for two servings; out of shell, about ¾ pound. Scallops or crab out of shell, about ¾ pound for two people; for crab in shell, plan on 2 to 3 pounds crab. Sixteen to 24 clams or oysters make a meal for two.

Barbecued Salmon Fillet

 Heat coals: 35 minutes. Preparation time: 10 minutes. Cooking time: 10 minutes per inch of fish thickness

Fresh salmon fillets are delicious barbecued with a baste of butter, wine, lemon juice, and soy sauce. Add corn-on-the-cob and juicy sliced tomatoes to complete this simple meal.

- ¾ to 1-pound salmon fillet
- 2 tablespoons butter or margarine, melted
- ¼ cup rosé or dry white wine
- 2 tablespoons *each* lemon juice and soy sauce
  Parsley and lemon wedges

Ignite coals about 35 minutes before you intend to begin cooking (you will need about 20 to 30 long-burning briquets). When coals are covered with gray ash, arrange in a single layer to underlie area being used on grill. Knock ash off coals. Adjust grill to 4 to 6 inches above low-glowing coals. Cut heavy-duty foil the same size as fish fillet. Place fillet, skin side down, on foil.

Combine butter, wine, lemon juice, and soy sauce. Place fish on grill, foil side down, and brush generously with butter sauce. Cover barbecue with its hood (or fashion a hood out of heavy-duty foil and place on grill to enclose fish). Cook, basting with butter sauce about every 5 minutes, until fish flakes readily when prodded in thickest portion with a fork (allow about 10 minutes cooking time for each inch of thickness).

To serve, slide fish, still on foil, onto a serving plate or board. Garnish with parsley and lemon. Slice fish to the skin and lift each serving away from skin. Reheat any remaining butter sauce and pass at table to serve over fish.

Salmon Ramekins with Hollandaise

 Preparation time: 10 minutes. Cooking time: 15 minutes

Attractively presented in individual ramekins, this salmon with hollandaise is made with ingredients that are easily kept on hand in cupboard and freezer. You can put it together on a moment's notice.

- 1 package (9 or 10 oz.) frozen Italian green beans
  Boiling salted water
- 1 can (about 8 oz.) salmon, drained
- 1 can (6 oz.) hollandaise sauce or ¾ cup homemade hollandaise
- ¼ teaspoon grated lemon peel
- ⅛ teaspoon tarragon, crumbled
- 2 tablespoons sliced or slivered blanched almonds

(Continued on next page)

Cook beans as directed on the package in boiling salted water until just tender; drain. Break salmon into large chunks, remove and discard bones and skin. Lightly butter two individual ramekins (1 to 1½ cups *each*) and spoon in beans and salmon chunks. Mix together hollandaise, lemon peel, and tarragon; spoon equal amounts of sauce over salmon and beans. Sprinkle with almonds. Bake in a 350° oven for about 15 minutes or until hot through.

Fillet of Sole Bonne Femme

 Preparation time: 10 minutes. Cooking time: 20 minutes

Delicately flavored sole cooked in white wine and cream makes a classic fish dish for two. Serve it with buttered green beans or lightly cooked zucchini.

- **4 sole fillets (¾ to 1 lb. total)**
  Salt and pepper
- **1 green onion, sliced (include some green tops)**
- **½ lemon, thinly sliced**
- **⅓ cup dry white wine**
  Water
- **2 tablespoons butter or margarine**
- **¼ pound mushrooms, sliced**
- **2 teaspoons all-purpose flour**
- **1 egg yolk**
- **2 tablespoons whipping cream**
  Chopped parsley and lemon wedges

Sprinkle sole lightly with salt and pepper. Fold fillets crosswise and place in a greased 8-inch-square baking pan. Top with onion and lemon slices; pour wine over all. Cover and bake in a 400° oven for 15 to 20 minutes or until fish flakes easily when prodded in thickest portion with a fork. Remove from oven; discard lemon slices. Drain pan liquid into a measuring cup; add water, if necessary, to make ½ cup. Keep sole warm.

Melt butter in a small pan over medium-high heat; add mushrooms and cook until lightly browned. Stir in flour until bubbly. Gradually add cooking liquid from fish and cook, stirring constantly, until thickened. In a bowl, combine egg yolk with cream and beat; stir in a little of the hot liquid from mushrooms. Add egg mixture to mushroom sauce in pan and cook, stirring constantly, until thickened.

Lift sole onto a warm serving dish. Blend a little of the liquid that collected in fish pan into mushroom sauce to thin it slightly, if needed. Spoon sauce over fish. Serve immediately, garnished with chopped parsley and lemon wedges.

Red Snapper Stew

 Preparation time (cooking included): 20 minutes

Red snapper and vegetables simmer in a savory tomato broth, ready to serve in minutes with French bread for dipping into the broth.

- **3 tablespoons olive oil or salad oil**
- **1 clove garlic, minced or pressed**
- **1 large onion, chopped**
- **1 green pepper, seeded and chopped**
- **1 can (8 oz.) tomatoes**
- **1 can (12 oz.) tomato juice**
- **½ teaspoon salt**
- **¼ cup dry white wine (or 1 tablespoon lemon juice and 3 tablespoons water)**
- **½ teaspoon oregano leaves**
- **1 teaspoon Worcestershire**
- **1 pound boned and skinned red snapper or other rockfish, cut in 1½-inch cubes**

In a 3 to 4-quart pan, heat oil over medium heat. Add garlic, onion, and green pepper; cook, stirring occasionally, until onion is limp. Add tomatoes (break them up with a spoon) and their liquid. Stir in tomato juice, salt, wine, oregano, and Worcestershire; bring to a boil. Add red snapper, then cover and simmer, stirring occasionally, until fish flakes easily when prodded with a fork (about 8 minutes).

Trout with Almonds

 Preparation time: 5 minutes. Cooking time: 10 minutes per inch of fish thickness

Butter-toasted almonds are sprinkled over sautéed trout just before serving. (See photograph on facing page.)

- **4 tablespoons butter or margarine**
- **4 to 8 tablespoons sliced almonds**
- **2 medium-size trout (about ½ lb. *each*)**
  Salt (optional)
- **1 tablespoon *each* lemon juice and chopped parsley**

In a wide frying pan over medium heat, melt 2 tablespoons of the butter and add almonds. Cook, stirring, until nuts are toasted golden. Pour nuts and butter from pan into a container and set aside.

(Continued on page 60)

BUTTER-TOASTED ALMOND SLIVERS blanket trout quickly sautéed at the last minute (recipe above). Plan on one or two trout per person for this meal in minutes.

58 SEAFOOD

...Trout with Almonds (cont'd.)

In same pan, melt remaining 2 tablespoons butter over medium-high heat and add fish. Cook until browned lightly on 1 side. Add more butter, if needed, and turn fish over with a wide spatula. Cook second side until lightly browned and fish flakes readily when prodded with a fork in thickest portion (allow 10 minutes—5 minutes each side—total cooking time for each 1 inch of thickness). Sprinkle fish lightly with salt, if desired.

Sprinkle reserved almonds on fish, then spoon over lemon juice and parsley.

Tuna Turnover

🕐 *Preparation time: 20 minutes. Cooking time: 20 minutes*

Puffy pastry is filled with a crunchy tuna salad mixture to make one big turnover. While it bakes, sip hot beef-flavored tomato cocktail topped with freshly ground pepper and lime juice. Count on 1 to 1½ cups for each of you.

    Pastry for single-crust 9-inch pie
2 **tablespoons butter or margarine, at room temperature**
1 **can (6½ oz.) chunk-style tuna, well drained**
⅓ **cup *each* thinly sliced green onion and celery**
⅓ **cup chopped dry roasted peanuts**
⅓ **cup sour cream**
1 **teaspoon lemon juice**
½ **teaspoon dill weed**
1 **red or green bell pepper, seeded and cut in rings**
    Dill pickle slices

Prepare your favorite pie pastry or use a packaged mix. Roll out dough on a lightly floured board into a 12-inch circle. Spread evenly with butter.

Combine tuna, onion, celery, peanuts, sour cream, lemon juice, and dill weed; spread mixture over half the dough to about 1 inch from edge. Fold unfilled half over the tuna mixture and crimp edges with tines of a fork to seal in filling.

With a wide spatula, transfer to an ungreased baking sheet; slash top in 2 or 3 places. Bake in a 425° oven, uncovered, for about 20 minutes or until golden brown. Remove to serving platter; garnish with pepper rings and dill pickles. Serve at once.

Sole with Asparagus

🕐 *Preparation time: 10 minutes. Cooking time: 6 to 9 minutes*

Bright green asparagus gives color and crunch to sole strips quickly stir-fried with garlic. Another time, try

this quick entrée with shelled and deveined shrimp; to avoid overcooking, remove shrimp from the pan as soon as they turn pink. Accompany with rice (or hot buttered noodles, if you prefer). Serve velvety Caramel Custard (page 76) for a sweet finale.

2 **teaspoons *each* cornstarch and soy sauce**
    Salad oil
¾ **pound sole fillets, cut in 1 by 3-inch strips**
1 **large clove garlic, minced or pressed**
1 **pound asparagus (tough ends removed), cut in ½-inch-thick slanting slices**
2 **tablespoons water**

In a small bowl, stir together cornstarch, soy, and 2 teaspoons oil. Gently stir in fish strips, coating pieces evenly.

Heat 2 tablespoons oil in a wok or wide frying pan over medium-high heat. When oil is hot, add fish and gently stir-fry until golden (2 to 3 minutes); remove from pan and set aside.

Increase heat to high. Add 1 more tablespoon oil to pan. When oil is hot, add garlic and stir once; then add asparagus and stir-fry for 1 minute. Add water; cover and cook for 2 to 3 minutes. Return fish to pan and stir-fry just until heated through.

Shrimp with Broccoli

Follow directions for **Sole with Asparagus,** but substitute ¾ pound raw **shrimp,** shelled and deveined, for sole. Stir-fry shrimp just until pink. Substitute ¾ pound **broccoli** for asparagus (cut off flowerets and slash their stems; peel any thick stems). Cook broccoli for 3 to 4 minutes after adding water.

60   SEAFOOD

juice, and onion. Spoon sauce over fish and spinach. Sprinkle with remaining 3 tablespoons cheese.

Bake, uncovered, in a 425° oven for about 15 minutes or until bubbly and lightly browned. Garnish with chopped parsley.

Scampi

Preparation time: 10 minutes. Cooking time: 6 minutes

For a quick version of the heady garlic-flavored scampi served in many Italian restaurants, try these shrimp sautéed with lemon juice and garlic. Rice makes a good accompaniment.

- **6 tablespoons butter or margarine**
- **1 tablespoon minced green onion**
- **1 tablespoon olive oil or salad oil**
- **4 to 5 cloves garlic, minced or pressed**
- **2 teaspoons lemon juice**
- **¼ teaspoon salt**
  About ¾ pound medium-size shrimp, shelled (but tails intact) and deveined
- **¼ teaspoon grated lemon peel**
- **2 tablespoons minced parsley**
  Dash liquid hot pepper seasoning
  Lemon wedges

Melt butter in a wide frying pan over medium heat. Stir in onion, oil, garlic, lemon juice, and salt; cook until bubbly. Add shrimp to pan and cook, stirring occasionally, until shrimp turn pink (about 5 minutes). Stir in lemon peel, parsley, and hot pepper seasoning; turn into serving dish. Garnish with lemon wedges to squeeze over each serving.

Scampi for one. Use 2 tablespoons **butter** or margarine; 1½ teaspoons minced **green onion;** 1½ teaspoons **olive oil** or salad oil; 2 cloves **garlic,** minced or pressed; 1 teaspoon **lemon juice;** ⅛ teaspoon **salt;** 6 ounces **shrimp;** ⅛ teaspoon grated **lemon peel;** 1 tablespoon minced **parsley;** and a dash of **liquid hot pepper seasoning.**

Sole Florentine

Preparation time: 15 minutes. Cooking time: 15 minutes

Rolled fillets of sole bake in a creamy sauce atop a bed of spinach. Use a shallow baking dish or individual ramekins.

- **4 sole fillets (¾ to 1 lb. total)**
- **1 bottle (8 oz.) clam juice**
- **1 package (10 oz.) frozen chopped spinach, thawed**
- **4 tablespoons grated Parmesan cheese**
- **2 tablespoons butter or margarine**
- **2 tablespoons all-purpose flour**
- **⅔ cup milk**
- **⅛ teaspoon ground nutmeg**
- **¼ teaspoon dry mustard**
- **1 tablespoon *each* lemon juice and instant minced onion**
  Chopped parsley

Loosely roll each fillet and secure with a pick. In a pan bring clam juice to a boil; set in sole, cover, and simmer for 3 to 5 minutes or until opaque white. Remove fish and drain. Boil clam juice, uncovered, until reduced to ½ cup; pour into cup and set aside.

Meanwhile, drain spinach well; distribute over bottom of a shallow 1-quart baking dish or 2 individual ramekins. Sprinkle evenly with 1 tablespoon of the Parmesan. Remove picks and arrange fish on spinach. Melt butter in pan over medium heat, blend in flour, and cook, stirring, until bubbly. Remove from heat and gradually stir in milk and clam juice; cook and stir until thickened. Add nutmeg, mustard, lemon

Shrimp and Mushroom Ramekins

Preparation time: 10 minutes. Cooking time: 22 minutes

Individual servings of cheese-blanketed shrimp bake with golden mushroom slices in a rich cream sauce while you prepare an accompanying green vegetable such as zucchini, broccoli, or green beans. Consider a light dessert of caramel custard (page 76).

(Continued on page 63)

- 4 tablespoons butter or margarine
- ¾ pound medium-size shrimp, shelled and deveined
- ¼ pound mushrooms, sliced
- 2 tablespoons chopped green onion
- 2 tablespoons all-purpose flour
- ⅛ teaspoon Dijon mustard
- ⅓ cup regular-strength chicken broth
- ¼ cup whipping cream
- 2 tablespoons dry sherry
  Salt and pepper
- ½ cup shredded Swiss cheese

Melt 2 tablespoons of the butter in a frying pan over medium heat; add shrimp and cook, stirring often, until shrimp turn pink (about 5 minutes). Transfer shrimp to 2 individual baking dishes.

To pan, add remaining 2 tablespoons butter, mushrooms, and green onion. Cook over medium heat, stirring, until mushrooms are golden brown; sprinkle in flour and cook until bubbly. Gradually stir in mustard, broth, and cream. Cook, stirring, until thickened and bubbly. Stir in sherry and salt and pepper to taste; spoon evenly over shrimp, and sprinkle with cheese. Bake, uncovered, in a 325° oven for 10 to 15 minutes or until hot through and cheese is melted.

Oven-fried Oysters

🕐 *Preparation time: 10 minutes. Cooking time: 12 minutes*

Rich, buttery, and crisply crusted, these baked oysters make a satisfying main dish accompanied by peas tossed with sliced celery lightly sautéed in butter. Serve a dessert of mint ice cream and cookies.

- About 16 saltine crackers
- 1 jar (10 oz.) small or medium-size oysters
- 6 tablespoons butter or margarine, melted
  Salt and pepper

Crush enough crackers to make ¾ cup fine crumbs. Spread ½ of the crumbs over bottom of a buttered 8 to 9-inch square baking dish. Drain oysters, then dip them into melted butter to coat well. Arrange oysters in a single layer over crumbs. Sprinkle lightly with salt and pepper to taste. Top with remaining crumbs.

IN A WOK, shrimp and scallops stir-fry quickly after marinating in teriyaki sauce (recipe at right). Add as many different sliced vegetables as your appetite desires.

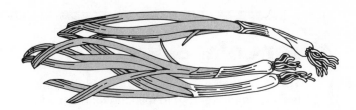

Drizzle remaining butter evenly over crumbs. Place baking dish on oven rack near top of oven. Bake, uncovered, in a 400° oven until crumbs on top are well browned (12 to 15 minutes). Serve immediately.

Shrimp-Scallop Teriyaki

🕐 *Preparation time: 15 minutes. Marinating time: 30 minutes. Cooking time: 5 minutes*

The luxury of stir-frying is that you can add ingredients to your heart's content. The photograph on page 62 suggests possibilities for varying this recipe with more vegetables—the quantity depends on your appetite. If you do add vegetables beyond what the recipe calls for, do so just before you add the seafood, stir-frying each additional quarter-pound of sliced vegetables in 1 to 2 more tablespoons of oil until just tender-crisp. (See photograph on facing page.)

- 4 tablespoons prepared teriyaki sauce
- 3 tablespoons dry sherry
- 1½ teaspoons finely chopped fresh ginger or ½ teaspoon ground ginger
- 2 cloves garlic, minced or pressed
- 1½ teaspoons cornstarch
- ½ pound medium-size shrimp, shelled and deveined
- ½ pound scallops, well rinsed
- 4 tablespoons peanut oil or salad oil
- ¼ pound edible-pod peas or 1 package (6 oz.) frozen pod peas, thawed and drained
- ½ pound mushrooms, sliced
- 5 green onions, cut in 2-inch lengths

Mix teriyaki sauce, sherry, ginger, garlic, and cornstarch in a deep container and add shrimp and scallops. Cover and refrigerate for at least ½ hour.

When ready to cook, assemble remaining ingredients so that you can reach them quickly. Pour 2 tablespoons of the oil into a wok or frying pan over high heat; when oil is hot, add peas and cook, stirring rapidly, until peas are bright green. Remove peas and set aside. Add remaining 2 tablespoons oil, heat again, and quickly stir and fry mushrooms. Pour in shrimp and scallops with their liquid; add onion and cook, stirring, over high heat until shrimp turn pink. Stir in reserved pod peas, remove from heat, and serve.

For Color & Verve, Think Vegetables

There's nothing like vegetables for adding color, texture, and taste—not to mention nutrition—to a meal. Cooked to just the right degree of doneness, they become the perfect partner for an entrée.

And because we know there will be times when you'll just want to steam your vegetables or cook them in a small amount of boiling water, we've included a chart that lists a number of favorite vegetables and the amount to buy when you're cooking for two.

You can figure quantities when you're buying fresh vegetables for one or two when you're dealing with one-apiece vegetables (maybe two-apiece, depending on your appetite) such as tomatoes, corn on the cob, potatoes, or artichokes. With others, though, you may need some guidance.

The trick is to approximate the amount of waste involved. Most fresh vegetables fall into one of two categories—those that, when purchased, are about half waste, and those with almost no waste. A general rule is that you'll need about a quarter-pound of *edible* vegetable per serving.

The recipes on these pages tell you how much to buy for two servings of these specific dishes. But when you just want to boil or steam a vegetable for simple presentation, use the following buying guide.

Vegetable	To Serve Two, Buy This Amount
Asparagus	1 pound
Beans, green or yellow wax	½ pound
Broccoli	⅔ to 1 pound
Brussels sprouts	½ pound
Carrots	½ pound
Mushrooms	½ pound
Parsnips	½ pound
Peas in shells	1 pound
Peas, edible pod	½ pound
Spinach	½ to ⅔ pound
Squash, summer (crookneck, patty pan, zucchini)	½ pound
Squash, winter (acorn, banana, butternut, Hubbard)	⅔ pound
Turnips	½ pound

Asparagus in Wine

Asparagus, cooked just until tender-crisp, is treated to a butter and wine sauce, then a dusting of Parmesan cheese. Special though it is, it takes only minutes.

> 1 pound asparagus
> Salted water
> 2 tablespoons butter or margarine
> 2 tablespoons dry white wine
> Salt and white pepper
> 3 tablespoons shredded Parmesan cheese

Snap off and discard tough ends from asparagus; wash asparagus. In a wide frying pan, bring ½ inch salted water to a boil. Add asparagus, cover, and cook over medium heat until tender-crisp when pierced (5 to 7 minutes). Drain well and turn into a shallow 3 to 4-cup casserole.

Melt butter in frying pan over high heat; add wine and cook, uncovered, until reduced by about half. Pour butter-wine sauce over asparagus. Sprinkle with salt and pepper to taste, then with cheese. Place under broiler, 2 to 3 inches from heat, until cheese melts (about 2 minutes).

Gingered Carrots with Sesame

The sweetness of carrots comes forth when they cook, and the freshness of ginger amplifies this sweetness. Garnish the carrot sticks with sesame seeds toasted to a nutlike flavor. (See photograph on page 31.)

> 1 tablespoon sesame seeds
> 6 medium-size carrots
> ¼ cup boiling salted water
> 2 tablespoons butter or margarine
> 1½ teaspoons minced candied ginger or grated fresh ginger, or ¾ teaspoon ground ginger
> Chopped parsley

Toast sesame seeds in a frying pan over medium heat until golden, stirring frequently. Set aside.

Peel carrots and cut into slender sticks about 3 inches long. Place in a pan with boiling salted water. Cover and cook over medium heat until just tender (8 to 10 minutes); drain. Add butter and ginger and cook, stirring, until carrots are glazed. To serve, sprinkle with reserved toasted sesame seeds and parsley.

Posh Squash

Bright yellow crookneck squash makes a colorful casserole topped with cheese. It is especially appealing with barbecued meats.

About ¾ pound crookneck squash
Boiling salted water
1 egg
⅓ cup mayonnaise
¼ cup finely chopped onion
2 tablespoons chopped green pepper
⅛ teaspoon thyme leaves
Salt and pepper
⅓ cup grated Parmesan cheese
½ tablespoon butter or margarine

Cut off and discard stem and blossom ends from squash; scrub squash but do not peel. Cut into ½-inch-thick slices and cook, covered, in a small amount of boiling salted water until just tender when pierced (3 to 5 minutes), drain well and set aside.

Beat egg, then blend in mayonnaise, onion, green pepper, and thyme. Stir in squash and add salt and pepper to taste.

Spoon mixture into a greased shallow 1-quart casserole; sprinkle evenly with cheese and dot with butter. Cover and chill if made ahead. Bake, uncovered, in a 375° oven for 20 minutes (25 minutes if refrigerated) or until puffed and lightly browned.

Baked Stuffed Eggplant

A Turkish delight, baked eggplant is well suited for lamb dishes. For a Middle-Eastern touch, serve unflavored yogurt to spoon over both eggplant and accompanying meat. The eggplant takes time to bake, but you can make it ahead and then serve it at room temperature. (See photograph on page 39.)

1 small eggplant (about ¾ lb.)
Salt
3 tablespoons olive oil or salad oil
1 medium-size onion, thinly sliced
2 small cloves garlic, minced or pressed
¼ cup minced parsley
½ teaspoon sugar
¾ teaspoon salt
1 large tomato, peeled, seeded, and diced
2 tablespoons pine nuts

Cut eggplant in half lengthwise and scoop out center, leaving a firm ½-inch-thick shell; reserve pulp.

Sprinkle shells lightly with salt. Use 1 tablespoon of the oil to grease a shallow baking pan; arrange eggplant in pan, skin side down.

Place remaining 2 tablespoons oil in a wide frying pan over medium-high heat; add onion and cook until limp. Stir in about 1 cup reserved eggplant pulp (diced), garlic, parsley, sugar, the ¾ teaspoon salt, and tomato. Evenly distribute filling in eggplant shells.

Place pine nuts on a shallow rimmed baking sheet. Bake in a 350° oven for 8 to 10 minutes or until toasted. Set aside.

Cover eggplant pan with foil and bake in a 350° oven for about 1 hour or until tender. Sprinkle with toasted pine nuts and serve hot or at room temperature.

Spinach Soufflé-stuffed Mushrooms

Bright green puffs of spinach soufflé nestle in large mushroom caps for a vegetable side dish that is good-tasting and elegant. (See photograph on page 31.)

6 mushrooms, *each* at least 2 inches in diameter
2 tablespoons butter or margarine
½ pound spinach
Dash of garlic powder
1 egg
1 tablespoon all-purpose flour
About 2 tablespoons grated Parmesan cheese

Remove stems from mushrooms; reserve for other uses. Melt 1 tablespoon of the butter in a wide frying pan over medium heat. Turn mushroom caps over in butter and arrange in a greased baking pan, cup side up; set aside.

Remove stems from spinach; wash leaves well. Add spinach, with water that clings to leaves, to frying pan; cook over medium heat until wilted (about 3 minutes). Press out all liquid. Whirl garlic powder and egg in a blender until egg is frothy; add spinach and whirl until smooth.

Melt remaining 1 tablespoon butter in frying pan, add flour, and cook, stirring, until bubbly; remove from heat and stir in spinach mixture.

Spoon equal amounts of spinach mixture into each mushroom cap. Sprinkle evenly with Parmesan cheese. Bake, uncovered, in a 400° oven for 10 to 15 minutes or until cheese is golden and soufflé puffy. Serve immediately.

Crab Vermouth

 Preparation time: 10 minutes. Cooking time: 20 minutes

Crab's delicate flavor needs only a simple presentation to be at its best. Here it is enhanced by a light but well-seasoned broth with overtones of dry vermouth and garlic. It is so easy to make—just heat cooked cracked crab in the broth and ladle it into serving bowls. Serve with crusty French bread for dunking.

- ¼ cup butter or margarine
- 1 tablespoon cornstarch (optional)
- 1 cup regular-strength chicken broth
- ½ cup dry vermouth
- 1 tablespoon chopped parsley
- 2 cloves garlic, minced or pressed
- 1½ teaspoons *each* soy sauce and lemon juice
- ½ teaspoon sugar
- 1 large (about 2 lbs.) cooked crab, cleaned and cracked
- 2 tablespoons dry vermouth
  Hot French bread

Melt butter in a wide frying pan over medium heat. If you want a slightly thickened broth, remove butter from heat and blend in cornstarch.

Gradually stir in chicken broth and the ½ cup dry vermouth. Add parsley, garlic, soy sauce, lemon juice, and sugar. Bring to a boil, reduce heat, cover, and simmer for 10 minutes.

To hot broth, add crab; cover and simmer until crab is heated through (about 10 minutes). Pour the 2 tablespoons dry vermouth over crab.

Ladle into shallow bowls. Serve with French bread for dunking.

Spaghetti with Clam Sauce

 Preparation time: 10 minutes. Cooking time: 18 minutes

Fresh clams lace the spaghetti sauce flavored with garlic, white wine, and plenty of parsley. Add garlic bread or bread sticks and a salad with marinated artichoke hearts for a complete meal.

- 16 fresh clams in the shell, well scrubbed
- ½ cup water
- 1 tablespoon butter or margarine
- ¼ pound spaghetti
- 2 cloves garlic, minced or pressed
- 2 shallots, minced
- ½ cup dry white wine
- 1 tablespoon cornstarch blended with 1 tablespoon water
- ¼ cup minced parsley

Place clams in a pot that they fill about halfway. Add water, cover, and simmer for about 8 minutes or until shells open; discard any unopened clams. Lift pan from heat and remove clams from their shells. Return clams to liquid in pan; discard shells.

Prepare spaghetti according to package directions.

Melt butter in a wide frying pan over medium-low heat. Add garlic and shallots and cook, uncovered, until limp but not brown (3 to 4 minutes). Add wine and clam liquid; simmer, uncovered, for about 5 minutes to blend flavors. Add cornstarch mixture and cook, stirring constantly, until bubbling. Remove from heat, pour in clams and any remaining liquid, then stir in parsley.

Drain spaghetti, mix in clam sauce, and serve at once.

Clams Bordelaise

 Cook rice ahead. Preparation time: 10 minutes. Cooking time: 7 minutes

Named for the white Bordeaux wine originally used to flavor the broth, clams bordelaise can be made with any dry white wine—or with lemon juice. Serve the clams, rice, and broth in a broad shallow soup bowl with a spoon and fork. A simple salad, classic bread sticks, and dry white wine provide a French-style meal. (See photograph on facing page.)

- 2 tablespoons butter or margarine
- 2 tablespoons finely chopped parsley
- 1 clove garlic, minced or pressed
  About 1 cup regular-strength chicken broth
- ½ cup dry white wine (or 2 tablespoons lemon juice with ⅓ cup regular-strength chicken broth)
- 16 fresh clams in the shell, well scrubbed
- 1 cup hot cooked rice

Melt butter in a 3-quart pan over medium heat. Add parsley and garlic and cook for 1 to 2 minutes. Pour in chicken broth and wine and bring to a boil. Add clams, cover, and cook over medium heat until clams open (5 to 10 minutes), adding more broth, if desired. Discard any unopened clams. To serve, spoon some of the hot rice into wide shallow bowls, arrange opened clams in each, then pour over broth and serve.

FIRESIDE DINNER FOR TWO includes steamed clams, crunchy sesame seed bread sticks, and chilled white wine. Clams cook in a flavorful broth of wine and garlic laden with rice in just a matter of minutes (recipe above). Accompany with grapes or other fruit.

EGGS & CHEESE

Eggs are a food for all seasons—and for all hours of the day and night. What's more, they usually are present in even the most barren refrigerator, ready for any presentation from simple to elegant.

Cheese is a good partner for eggs in spur-of-the-moment meals. It, too, is convenient to keep on hand, and it is available in impressive variety.

Put the two together according to the recipes that follow, and you get quiches, soufflés, egg enchiladas, omelets—all perfect answers when you're looking for something light and lovely to cook.

Cheese Soufflé

 Preparation time: 10 minutes. Cooking time: 18 minutes

A soufflé, the aristocrat of the egg family, can be assembled in minutes. You should be ready to sit down and eat as soon as it's out of the oven, though it will hold in the oven for about 5 minutes before falling. Bake it in individual soufflé dishes or one larger dish. Serve a favorite salad while the soufflé bakes, then accompany your masterpiece with a green vegetable, such as broccoli spears.

    1 tablespoon butter or margarine
    1 tablespoon all-purpose flour
   ⅓ cup milk
       Dash of cayenne pepper
   ⅛ teaspoon dry mustard
   ¾ cup shredded sharp Cheddar cheese
    2 tablespoons grated Parmesan cheese
    2 eggs, separated

In a pan over medium heat, melt butter, stir in flour, and cook, stirring, until bubbly. Remove from heat and gradually stir in milk; add cayenne and mustard. Cook, stirring, until thick. Add Cheddar cheese and 1 tablespoon of the Parmesan; stir over heat until cheese melts. Remove cheese mixture from heat and beat in egg yolks. Beat egg whites until they hold distinct but moist peaks; carefully fold into cheese mixture.

Butter well a 3 to 4-cup soufflé dish or 2 individual 1¼-cup soufflé dishes; coat inside with remaining 1 tablespoon Parmesan cheese. Pour in soufflé mixture and with the tip of a knife, draw a circle on top surface about 1 inch inside rim. Bake in a 350° oven until soufflé feels firm when lightly tapped and crack looks fairly dry (about 18 to 20 minutes for a 1-quart dish, 12 to 15 minutes for individual dishes).

Onion Soufflé

 Preparation time: 15 minutes. Cooking time: 18 minutes

Onions, used discreetly, give a mildly robust flavor to a soufflé that is good with any simply cooked meat or fish. Baked in individual soufflé dishes, it would add special flair to a patio supper featuring barbecued steaks.

    2 tablespoons butter or margarine
    1 medium-size onion, chopped
   1½ tablespoons all-purpose flour
   ¼ teaspoon salt
       Dash of thyme leaves, crumbled
       Dash of white pepper
   ⅓ cup milk
    3 eggs, separated

Melt butter in a pan over medium heat; add onion and cook until soft and lightly browned. Stir in flour, salt, thyme, and pepper and cook until bubbly. Remove from heat and gradually stir in milk. Cook, stirring, until very thick. Whirl in blender or food processor until smooth.

Return sauce to pan and heat to simmering, stirring. Remove from heat and beat in egg yolks. Heat and stir for a few seconds or until thick again; remove from heat. Whip egg whites until they hold short, distinct, moist peaks. Fold half the whites thoroughly into sauce, then fold in remaining whites.

Pour into well-buttered individual 1¼-cup soufflé dishes or a 3 to 4-cup soufflé dish. Bake in a 375° oven for about 18 to 20 minutes or until brown. Serve immediately.

Baked Egg and Tomato Ramekins

Preparation time: 5 minutes. Cooking time: 35 minutes

The affinity of eggs and tomatoes is evident in this tempting egg dish baked in individual casseroles. Serve them for a leisurely weekend brunch with sausage links and toasted English muffins.

 1 **can (about 14 oz.) stewed tomatoes, drained**
 2 **tablespoons butter or margarine**
 ½ **cup sliced green onion**
 ¼ **pound mushrooms, sliced**
 1 **tablespoon all-purpose flour**
 ¼ **teaspoon *each* dry basil and garlic salt**
    Dash *each* pepper and sugar
 3 **tablespoons grated Parmesan cheese**
 2 **eggs**
    Chopped parsley

With a spoon, press tomatoes gently in a wire strainer to remove remaining liquid (save for other uses); set tomatoes aside.

In a pan, melt 1 tablespoon of the butter. Add onion and mushrooms. Cook, uncovered, over medium-high heat, stirring frequently, until juices evaporate.

Add remaining 1 tablespoon butter, melt, and stir in flour; cook, stirring, until bubbly. Add tomatoes, basil, garlic salt, pepper, and sugar. Cook, stirring and breaking up large tomato pieces, until sauce thickens (about 5 minutes).

Blend in 1 tablespoon of the Parmesan cheese. Divide tomato sauce between 2 buttered ramekins (about 1-cup size). Break 1 egg into each. Bake, uncovered, in a 325° oven for 25 minutes for soft-cooked eggs, 30 minutes for firm-cooked. Sprinkle evenly with remaining 2 tablespoons grated Parmesan cheese and chopped parsley.

Scrambled Egg Pizza

Preparation time (cooking included): 15 minutes

Scrambled eggs make a fluffy "crust" for this savory pizza. Add bread sticks and a marinated bean salad to complete a fast skillet dinner for a busy evening.

 4 **eggs**
 ¼ **cup sour cream**
 ¼ **teaspoon *each* salt and liquid hot pepper seasoning**
    Dash of pepper
 1½ **tablespoons butter or margarine**
 ¼ **cup *each* shredded Swiss and grated Parmesan cheese**
 ½ **teaspoon oregano leaves, crumbled**
 3 **green onions, thinly sliced**
 4 **cherry tomatoes, halved**
 3 **thin slices salami, cut in strips**
 2 **anchovies (optional)**

Beat together eggs, sour cream, salt, hot pepper seasoning, and pepper until blended. Melt butter in small frying pan over medium-low heat. When butter begins to foam, add eggs. Cook, uncovered, lifting cooked portion with a wide spatula to allow uncooked egg to flow under. When eggs are just softly set, remove from heat.

Sprinkle cheeses evenly over eggs; then sprinkle oregano evenly over cheese. Broil about 4 inches from heat just until cheese is melted. Distribute onion over eggs; arrange cherry tomatoes, salami, and anchovies (if used) on top of onion. Cut in wedges.

Individual Omelets

 Preparation time (cooking included): 10 minutes

You can turn out individual omelets for one or two people in a very few minutes, once you know how—and it's not difficult to master the technique. You'll need an omelet pan, or any fairly heavy frying pan with sloping sides. For a two or three-egg omelet, a 7 or 8-inch-diameter pan is best. There are endless filling choices; several are given below.

> 2 or 3 eggs
> ¼ teaspoon salt
> Dash of pepper
> 1 tablespoon water
> ½ to 1 tablespoon butter or margarine
> Filling (optional; suggestions follow)

For each omelet, break eggs into a small bowl and add salt, pepper, and water. Beat just enough to mix yolks and whites.

Place an omelet pan (or heavy pan with flaring rim and sloping sides) over medium-high heat. To the hot pan add butter and heat until foam begins to subside. Pour in egg mixture all at once. As soon as edges of egg start to turn opaque, slide a spatula under them, lifting so liquid portion runs underneath. Gently shake pan to keep omelet free. Continue to shake pan and lift omelet edges until there is no more liquid but the top still looks moist and creamy.

Sprinkle 2 to 3 tablespoons filling (1 or a combination from suggestions that follow) onto omelet, in line with pan handle. Holding pan in your left hand, slide spatula under right edge of omelet; lift and fold over about ⅓ of omelet. Switch pan to your right hand and tilt over a warm serving plate. Gently shake pan to slide unfolded edge of omelet just onto plate. Flick your right wrist downward so that folded edge of omelet, guided by spatula, falls neatly over omelet edge on plate. Makes 1 serving.

Fillings. Choose 1 or more from this list: shredded **cheese** (jack, Cheddar, or Parmesan); thinly sliced **spinach leaves;** diced **avocado; alfalfa sprouts;** sliced **mushrooms** (raw or sautéed in butter); freshly cooked or canned crumbled **bacon bits;** thinly sliced **ham; salami** slivers; small cooked **shrimp** (or flaked crab or tuna); salted **roasted sunflower seeds;** diced **tomato.**

OPEN-FACED COUNTRY OMELET for two is topped with diced and sautéed potato pieces, crisp bacon, Swiss cheese, parsley, and sautéed walnut halves. Garnish with cream; cut in wedges to serve (recipe at right).

Country Omelet

 Preparation time (cooking included): 20 minutes

The toppings for this open-faced omelet are an effective contrast of both flavors and textures: crunchy bacon, bits of cooked potato and onion, chewy cheese, cool sour cream, and crisp sautéed walnuts. (See photograph on facing page.)

> 4 slices bacon
> About 8 walnut halves
> 1 small diced new potato (about ⅛-inch pieces)
> ¼ cup diced onion
> 2 tablespoons butter or margarine
> 3 to 4 eggs, slightly beaten
> ¼ cup diced (about ⅛-inch pieces) Swiss cheese
> 2 tablespoons shredded Swiss cheese
> 1 tablespoon minced parsley
> About ¼ cup sour cream
> Salt

In a wide frying pan, cook bacon over medium heat until crisp and browned. Lift out bacon, break into pieces, and set aside. To drippings, add walnuts and cook, stirring, over medium heat 1 to 2 minutes or until lightly browned; set nuts aside. Discard all but 2 tablespoons drippings. Add potatoes and onions and cook, stirring, over medium-low heat until potatoes are soft to bite but only slightly browned (about 10 minutes); remove from pan and set aside; keep warm or reheat.

Clean frying pan to remove any browned particles, then melt butter over medium-low heat. Pour in eggs, pushing them from bottom as they set, allowing uncooked portion to flow down under. When top of omelet is almost set but still a little liquid-looking, sprinkle evenly with potatoes, diced cheese, bacon pieces, shredded cheese, and parsley. Mound sour cream in center of omelet. Garnish with toasted walnuts. Cut into wedges to serve. Salt to taste.

Sausage Scramble

Preparation time (cooking included): 15 minutes

Another good idea for a quick dinner is this interpretation of the classic Western favorite, Joe's Special. Instead of the traditional spinach-ground beef mixture, Italian sausage and Swiss chard team up. Serve it with French bread and butter, and a dry red wine.

> 2 mild Italian sausages (6 to 8 oz. total)
> 1 small onion, chopped
> 1 clove garlic, minced or pressed
> 2 cups finely shredded Swiss chard leaves
> 3 eggs
> Tomato wedges
> Grated Parmesan cheese

(Continued on page 72)

Remove casings from sausages and crumble meat into a small frying pan. Cook, uncovered, over medium-high heat until lightly browned. Add onion and garlic; cook, stirring, until onion is limp. Stir chard leaves into pan (reserve stems for other uses); cook, stirring, until chard is wilted and bright green (about 1 minute). Remove from heat.

Beat eggs until blended; pour over chard mixture and cook over low heat, stirring often, until eggs are just set. Spoon mixture onto warm serving plates. Accompany with tomato wedges and Parmesan cheese to sprinkle over individual servings.

Mexican Scrambled Eggs

⏰ *Preparation time (cooking included): 15 minutes*

Eggs scrambled with mushrooms top crisp cheese-sprinkled tortillas. They are good for brunch or a light supper with a green salad—and for dessert, coconut-strewn orange slices.

- **2 tablespoons butter or margarine**
- **¼ pound mushrooms, sliced**
- **¼ cup sliced green onion**
- **1 tablespoon seeded and chopped canned California green chiles**
- **2 flour tortillas**
- **1 cup (4 oz.) shredded Cheddar or jack cheese**
- **4 eggs**
- **¼ teaspoon salt**
- **1 small avocado, peeled, pitted, and sliced Red or green taco sauce**

Melt butter in a frying pan over medium heat. Add mushrooms, onion, and chiles; cook, uncovered, until mushrooms are limp and liquid has evaporated (about 5 minutes).

Meanwhile, arrange tortillas on a baking sheet; sprinkle evenly with cheese and place in a 350° oven until cheese is melted (about 4 minutes). Beat eggs and salt until blended; pour into mushroom mixture and cook, lifting cooked portion with a wide spatula to allow uncooked egg to flow under. Cook until done to your liking. Spoon eggs over cheese-topped tortillas; top with avocado slices. Pass taco sauce. Serve with knife and fork.

Florentine Spinach with Eggs

⏱ *Preparation time: 20 minutes. Cooking time: 8 minutes*

Egg yolks bake in a hollow of puffy egg white topping an individual serving of spinach and cheese. Serve this quickly made entrée for brunch, lunch, or a late supper.

- **1 package (10 oz.) frozen chopped spinach, thawed**
- **Dash of nutmeg**
- **2 tablespoons sour cream**
- **¼ teaspoon prepared mustard**
- **4 green onions, thinly sliced**
- **2 slices (2 oz. total) jack cheese**
- **4 eggs, separated**
- **½ teaspoon cream of tartar**
- **¼ teaspoon salt**

Put spinach into a wire strainer and press out liquid. Mix spinach, nutmeg, sour cream, and mustard. Divide between 2 greased 1¼ cup individual casseroles or soufflé dishes. Reserve half the onion; evenly distribute remaining onion over spinach mixture. Top each casserole with a slice of cheese. Bake in a 475° oven for 4 to 5 minutes or until heated through.

In a bowl beat egg whites, cream of tartar, and salt until eggs form stiff, distinct peaks.

Remove casseroles from oven and immediately cover with egg white topping. With spoon, make a ½-inch-deep depression in center of each and slip 2 egg yolks into each. Return to oven; continue to bake for 4 to 6 minutes, until topping begins to brown. Sprinkle remaining onion over tops.

Egg Enchiladas

⏱ *Preparation time: 15 minutes. Cooking time: 13 minutes*

For a quick enchilada filling, try eggs scrambled with green chiles. This dish makes a good meatless supper when you add an iceberg lettuce salad and warm refried beans topped with thinly sliced green onion.

1½ tablespoons salad oil
1 small onion, chopped
½ cup chopped green pepper
1 large can (15 oz.) tomato sauce
1½ teaspoons chili powder
5 eggs
2 tablespoons half-and-half (light cream) or milk
1½ tablespoons seeded, chopped canned California green chiles
Salt and pepper
1½ tablespoons butter or margarine
4 corn tortillas
¾ cup shredded Cheddar cheese

Heat oil in a frying pan over medium heat. Add onion and green pepper and cook, uncovered, until limp. Add tomato sauce and chili powder; simmer, uncovered, for about 10 minutes.

Beat eggs lightly with half-and-half; add chiles, and salt and pepper to taste.

Melt butter in frying pan over medium-low heat; add eggs and cook until softly set; keep warm.

Dip each tortilla in hot tomato sauce until soft; spoon ¼ of the scrambled eggs down center. Turn part of tortilla over filling, roll, and place seam side down in a shallow baking dish. Reheat remaining sauce to boiling, pour over top, and sprinkle with cheese. Place under broiler 4 inches from heat until cheese melts (about 3 minutes). Makes 2 servings of 2 enchiladas each.

Show-stopper Dutch Baby Pancake

Made with eggy batter like that used for popovers, this pancake puffs up dramatically in the oven. The results are especially spectacular when the batter is baked in a big container such as a paella pan. Whatever the shape of the pan, it should be fairly shallow—not much over 3 inches deep. Pick your pan; measure its total volume by pouring in quart measures of water.

Serve the pancake for breakfast, lunch, or supper. It's delicious with fruit topping either spooned over or served alongside.

For a 2 to 3-quart pan, use ¼ cup **butter** or margarine, 3 **eggs,** and ¾ cup *each* **milk** and **all-purpose flour.**

For a 3 to 4-quart pan, use ⅓ cup **butter** or margarine, 4 **eggs,** and 1 cup *each* **milk** and **all-purpose flour.**

Place butter in pan and set in a 425° oven. While butter melts, mix batter quickly.

Put eggs in a blender or food processor and whirl at high speed for 1 minute. With motor running, gradually pour in milk, then slowly add flour; continue whirling for 30 seconds.

Remove pan from oven, pour in batter, and bake until puffy and well browned (20 to 25 minutes, depending on pan size).

Dust pancake with **ground nutmeg,** if you wish, and serve at once with any of the following **toppings.** Makes 2 servings.

Pancake Toppings

Fresh fruit. Serve a bowl of sliced strawberries, sweetened to taste; or defrosted frozen peach slices; or any fruits in season, cut and sweetened.

Hot fruit. Sauté fresh apple or pear slices in a little butter or margarine until tender and translucent. Sweeten with sugar or honey to taste and offer with cinnamon-sugar and sour cream or yogurt. Or heat banana or papaya slices in melted butter or margarine over medium heat, turning, until hot; serve with lime wedges.

Canned pie filling. To cherry or apple pie filling, add lemon juice and ground cinnamon to taste. Serve cold or warmed, topped with yogurt or sour cream.

Powdered sugar. Have a shaker or bowl of powdered sugar and thick wedges of lemon at the table. Sprinkle sugar on hot pancake, then squeeze lemon over.

Syrups. Pass warm honey, maple syrup, or any favorite fruit syrup.

Cheese, Onion, and Chile Pie

⏱ *Preparation time: 20 minutes. Cooking time: 38 minutes*

Here is a cheese pie with a Mexican accent—sour cream, green chiles, and two mild cheeses. A good companion is a crisp green salad with cherry tomatoes and sliced avocado.

> **Buttery pastry shell (see crab quiche recipe, this page)**
> 2 **tablespoons butter or margarine**
> 1 **large onion, thinly sliced**
> 1 **cup sour cream**
> 2 **eggs**
> **Dash of salt**
> ¼ **cup seeded and chopped canned California green chiles**
> ⅔ **cup** *each* **shredded jack and Longhorn Cheddar cheese**

Prepare pastry shell. Melt butter in a small frying pan over medium heat. Add onion and cook, stirring, until limp and slightly browned (8 to 10 minutes); remove from heat and cool slightly.

Meanwhile, beat together sour cream, eggs, and salt; stir in chiles, cooled onion mixture, jack cheese, and ⅓ cup of the Cheddar. Spread filling in cooled pastry shell and bake in a 350° oven until filling is almost set (about 25 minutes). Sprinkle with remaining ⅓ cup Cheddar cheese, return to oven, and continue baking for 5 minutes longer or until custard is set when pan is jiggled. Let stand for a few minutes to cool slightly before cutting in wedges to serve.

Cheese Ramekins

⏱ *Preparation time: 10 minutes. Chilling time: 2 hours. Cooking time: 20 minutes*

This make-ahead brunch dish bears some resemblance to both a cheese fondue and a quiche. A white wine cheese custard saturates the buttered bread base and puffs it up when baked. Serve with link sausage and fruit.

> **Butter or margarine, at room temperature**
> 2 **slices white bread**
> 2 **eggs**
> 1 **cup half-and-half (light cream) or milk**
> ¼ **cup dry white wine**
> ⅛ **teaspoon** *each* **salt and dry mustard**
> 1½ **cups shredded Swiss cheese**
> 2 **thinly sliced green onions**

Spread butter on both sides of bread; place in shallow individual baking dishes (about 1-cup size). Beat eggs until light, then beat in half-and-half, wine, salt, and mustard. Evenly distribute cheese over bread, then pour egg mixture over, dividing evenly. Sprinkle onion slices over top. Cover and chill for at least 2 hours or until next day.

Bake, uncovered, in a 350° oven for 20 to 25 minutes or until custard appears set when jiggled.

Crab Quiche

⏱ *Preparation time: 20 minutes. Cooking time: 1 hour*

For brunch or a late evening supper, serve this crab quiche, elegant in its buttery pastry crust. Complement it with a well-chilled champagne or dry white wine. (See photograph on facing page.)

> **Buttery pastry shell (recipe follows)**
> ½ **cup shredded Swiss, Samsoe, or Gruyère cheese**
> 6 **ounces (about 1½ cups) cooked or canned crab meat, flaked and drained well**
> 3 **tablespoons** *each* **thinly sliced green onions, including some tops, and grated Parmesan cheese**
> 1 **tablespoon finely chopped parsley**
> ⅛ **teaspoon ground red pepper (cayenne)**
> **Dash of salt**
> 2 **eggs**
> ¾ **cup half-and-half (light cream)**
> **Paprika**

Prepare pastry shell; evenly sprinkle Swiss cheese over bottom of shell. In a small bowl, combine crab, onions, Parmesan cheese, parsley, pepper, and salt; spoon over Swiss cheese.

Beat eggs with half-and-half and pour over crab mixture. Sprinkle with paprika. Bake on lowest rack in a 350° oven for 45 minutes or until custard appears firm when dish is gently shaken. Let stand for 10 minutes, then cut in wedges to serve.

Buttery pastry shell. In a bowl, cut 5 tablespoons firm **butter** or margarine into ¾ cup **all-purpose flour** until mixture resembles fine crumbs. With a fork, lightly stir in 1 **egg yolk.** Work dough into a ball with your hands.

Using your fingers, evenly press dough over bottom and up sides of an 8-inch quiche dish or pie pan. Make dough flush with dish rim. Dough tears easily, but does not toughen with handling; pinch tears together to rejoin.

AN INTIMATE GARDEN PARTY features golden crab quiche, served hot or cold (recipe above) and avocado halves filled with Russian dressing. Let the champagne flow.

And in Conclusion...Desserts

Whether dessert for the two of you is an almost-always routine or an almost-never treat, you'll be intrigued by the possibilities for making special sweets on a small scale. Here we present ideas for lifting ice cream, puddings, and fruit from the mundane to the marvelous. And then there are the miniatures—little individual tarts, soufflés, even a cheesecake, sized to satisfy, not to overwhelm.

Meringue Heart Sundaes

For Valentine's day or any other romantic occasion, fill heart-shaped meringue shells with ice cream and top with a crimson fruit sauce.

With an electric mixer, beat 1 **egg white** and ⅛ teaspoon **cream of tartar** until very foamy. Gradually sprinkle in ¼ cup **sugar,** 1 tablespoon at a time, beating well after each addition. Beat until meringue holds very stiff peaks. Add ¼ teaspoon **vanilla;** beat for about 30 seconds longer.

Cover a baking sheet with baking parchment or brown wrapping paper. Draw 2 heart shapes, each 5 inches across at the widest point, on the paper. With a spatula or knife, spread meringue over heart shape, building up sides so they stand ½ to ¾ inch high.

Bake in a 275° oven for 45 minutes; then turn oven off and let meringue shells dry in oven for 1½ hours. Wrap each airtight if made ahead.

To serve, thaw 1 cup **unsweetened frozen strawberries** (crush a few to make some juice), then sweeten berries and juice to taste with **sugar.** (You can substitute strawberry-flavored ice cream topping.) Fill each meringue heart with a large scoop of **strawberry ice cream;** top with berry sauce.

Peppermint Tapioca Parfaits

Layer the minty pudding with chocolate cooky crumbs in parfait glasses for this pretty make-ahead dessert.

In a pan, mix 1½ tablespoons each **quick-cooking tapioca** and **sugar,** 1 cup **milk,** dash **salt,** and 1 **egg yolk;** let stand for 5 minutes. Beat 1 **egg white** until very foamy; then gradually sprinkle in 1 tablespoon **sugar,** beating until soft peaks form; set aside.

Cook tapioca mixture over medium heat, stirring constantly, until it comes to a full boil (about 6 to 8 minutes). Remove from heat and gently fold in beaten egg white just until blended. Stir in ½ teaspoon **vanilla** and a few drops **red food coloring,** if desired. Let cool, uncovered, for 30 minutes. Fold in 3 tablespoons crushed **peppermint candy.** Cover and chill. Meanwhile, crush enough **chocolate cookies** to make ⅓ cup crumbs.

To serve, place about 1 tablespoon crumbs in each of 2 parfait glasses (at least 1-cup size). Top with several spoonfuls tapioca mixture; repeat layers, ending with a sprinkling of crumbs. Cover and chill if made ahead. Garnish with mint sprigs, if desired.

One-Apple Pie

One good-sized apple, sliced and mixed with sugar and spice, makes one nice-sized apple pie for two.

First make pastry: In a bowl combine ⅓ cup **all-purpose flour** (unsifted), 1 teaspoon **sugar,** and 2 tablespoons **butter** or margarine; rub with fingers until evenly mixed. With a fork stir in 1 tablespoon **milk** until dough holds together. Press into a ball and cut in half. Roll out one portion on a floured board until large enough to fit a 4 to 5-inch pie pan. With some pastry extending beyond rim, fit pastry into pan.

Peel, core, and slice 1 medium-size Golden Delicious or Newton Pippin apple. Mix with 1 to 2 tablespoons sugar and ¼ teaspoon ground cinnamon. Pile fruit into pastry-lined pan. Roll out remaining pastry on floured board until large enough to cover apples. Fold pastry edges together to seal in fruit, then crimp rim. Prick top and sprinkle lightly with sugar.

Bake pie on lowest rack in a 375° oven for about 45 minutes or until crust is well browned. Let cool; serve slightly warm or cold.

Caramel Custard

Caramelized sugar coats the bottoms of the cups in which the custard bakes, creating a sauce.

In a small frying pan over medium heat, melt 2½ tablespoons **sugar,** shaking pan as sugar begins to liquefy and caramelize. When liquid (do not let scorch), pour at once, equally, into 2 small, deep individual baking dishes (*each* at least ¾-cup size).

In a bowl, beat until blended, but not frothy, 2 **eggs,** 2 tablespoons **sugar,** and ¼ teaspoon **vanilla.** Bring 1 cup **milk** to scalding and stir into eggs. Pour an equal portion into each baking dish.

Set dishes in a rimmed pan and place in a 350° oven; at once pour **boiling water** into pan to a depth of about 1 inch.

Bake for about 30 minutes or until center of custard jiggles only slightly when a dish is shaken gently. Lift from water at once and let cool. Serve at room temperature; or cover and chill for as long as 2 days.

Run a knife between custard and dish, then invert onto individual serving plates.

Fresh Raspberry Tarts

A tender press-in pastry enhances a filling of fresh berries. Bake the tart shells ahead and freeze them, if you like. (See photograph on page 18.)

From a total of 1½ cups **raspberries,** measure ½ cup and put in a blender or food processor. Add ¼ cup **sugar** and 2 tablespoons **water;** whirl until smooth. (If you wish, pour through a wire strainer and discard seeds.)

In a pan, blend puréed berries with 1 tablespoon **cornstarch.** Cook over medium-high heat, stirring constantly, until thickened and clear. Remove from heat and stir in ½ teaspoon **lemon juice** and a dash **ground nutmeg.** Gently mix in remaining 1 cup berries. Evenly spoon berry filling into **tart shells** (recipe follows) and serve hot, warm, or chilled. Top each tart with **whipped cream** or ice cream, if you like. Makes 2 tarts.

Tart shells. Mix ½ cup **all-purpose flour** (unsifted), 1 tablespoon **powdered sugar,** and a dash **salt.** With 2 knives cut in 3 tablespoons firm **butter** or margarine until mixture is uniformly crumbly. Stir 1 **egg yolk** into flour mixture, then use your hands to press dough together; divide into 2 equal parts. Press pastry evenly into 2 pie pans, each 4½ inches in diameter. Pierce bottom and sides all over with a fork. Bake in a 325° oven for 18 to 20 minutes or until golden brown. Cool in pans on a rack. Leave in tins or carefully remove shells to fill.

Individual Soufflés with Cherry Sauce

These fluffy little soufflés bake while you're eating the main course. Enjoy them hot from the oven, with a steaming cherry sauce poured over.

Butter 2 individual soufflé dishes (1-cup size) and sprinkle lightly with **sugar.** Beat 1 **egg white** until very foamy. Gradually sprinkle in 1½ tablespoons **sugar,** beating until stiff peaks form. In another bowl, stir together 1 **egg yolk,** ½ cup **sour cream,** 1½ tablespoons **sugar,** ½ teaspoon **grated lemon peel,** and a dash of **salt.** Fold into beaten egg white. Spoon mixture equally into soufflé dishes.

Bake in a 350° oven for 20 minutes or until soufflés jiggle only slightly when dishes are gently shaken; serve at once. Pass hot **cherry sauce** (recipe follows) to spoon over each.

Cherry sauce. Drain 1 small can (9 oz.) **pitted dark sweet cherries,** reserving syrup. In a pan, combine syrup, 1 tablespoon **sugar,** and 1½ teaspoons **cornstarch.** Cook, stirring, over medium-high heat, until sauce boils and thickens. Remove from heat, stir in cherries and ¼ teaspoon **brandy** or rum flavoring. Serve hot.

Cream Cheesecake

A 3-ounce cheesecake, split two ways, is everything your sweet tooth requires. Working with small quantities, you press in and bake a crust, then fill it with a cream cheese mixture.

In a small bowl, combine 3 tablespoons **all-purpose flour,** 1 tablespoon **sugar,** and 1 tablespoon **butter** or margarine. Rub between your fingers until evenly mixed. Turn into a greased 4½ to 5-inch-diameter round container and press firmly in bottom. Bake in a 325° oven for 15 to 20 minutes or until crust is lightly browned. Remove from oven.

While crust bakes, mash 1 small package (3 oz.) **cream cheese** (at room temperature) with a fork. Blend in 1 tablespoon **sugar,** ⅛ teaspoon grated **lemon peel,** ¼ teaspoon **vanilla,** and 1 **egg,** mixing well. Pour into baked crust. Bake in a 325° oven for 15 minutes or until filling appears set when pan is gently jiggled.

Meanwhile, mix 2 tablespoons **sour cream** and 1 teaspoon **sugar.** When you take cheesecake from oven, at once spread with sour cream mixture. Chill, then serve.

RECIPES FOR THE MICROWAVE

Microwave cooking might have been designed with a duo in mind—it works especially well with small portions of food. In this chapter, we offer a delectable array of entrées just for dining à *deux*. All recipes include complete microwave instructions, and many of the recipe introductions feature helpful tips.

We developed these recipes using a 650-watt microwave oven and four power designations: HIGH (100%)—600 to 650 watts; MEDIUM-HIGH (70%)—450 to 490 watts; MEDIUM (50%)—300 to 350 watts; and MEDIUM-LOW (30%)—180 to 210 watts.

Since cooking times will vary slightly depending on the utensils used, the temperature of the food before cooking, and the idiosyncrasies of your own oven, use the times in our recipes as a general guide.

Standing time and doneness tests are very important in microwave cooking. Food continues to cook after it's removed from the oven; let it stand for the recommended time before you check doneness. Then, if it's not done to your liking, microwave it further, in 30-second increments. It's better to undercook and add more cooking time later than to overcook.

GOLDEN OUTSIDE, JUICY WITHIN—the browning dish works its magic on Italian-style Chicken Scallops (page 83). Microwaved green beans (page 85) and pasta cooked on top of the range complete the meal.

Liver with Apples and Onions

🕐 Preparation time: 12 minutes.
Microwaving time: 15 minutes.
Standing time: 3 minutes.

Tender apple wedges, onions, and a sauce of sherry and cream transform quickly cooked liver into something special. For the most even cooking, choose sliced liver of uniform thickness; thin, tapered ends will overcook before a thicker center is done.

- 2 **tablespoons butter or margarine**
- 1 **small onion, chopped**
- ⅓ **cup whipping cream**
- 1 **tablespoon salad oil**
- ¾ **pound calf's liver, about ¼ inch thick, membrane removed, cut in serving-size pieces**
- ½ **cup dry sherry**
- 2 **teaspoons cornstarch**
- 1 **small Golden Delicious apple, cored and cut in ¼-inch-thick slices**

Place butter in a 1-quart microwave-proof bowl. Microwave, uncovered, on **HIGH (100%)** for 30 seconds or until melted. Add onion and microwave, uncovered, on **HIGH (100%)** for 5 minutes or until golden. Stir in cream; cover and set aside.

Microwave a 10-inch browning dish or skillet on **HIGH (100%)** for 4½ minutes. Carefully transfer dish (bottom will be very hot) to a heatproof surface. Add oil and tilt dish to coat bottom evenly. At once arrange liver in dish in a single layer, then slightly tilt dish so oil touches each liver piece (this helps pieces brown more evenly). Let stand until sizzling stops, then turn pieces over.

Sprinkle liver with 1 tablespoon of the sherry. Microwave, uncovered, on **HIGH (100%)** for 1 minute. Turn liver pieces over; bring pieces that look raw to outside of dish and push cooked ones to inside. Microwave on **HIGH (100%)**, uncovered, for 30 seconds. Liver should be very pink when slashed (it continues to cook upon standing). Transfer liver to a platter; cover and let stand for 3 minutes.

Meanwhile, wipe out browning dish. Stir cornstarch into remaining 7 tablespoons sherry; add to dish along with onion-cream mixture. Microwave, uncovered, on **HIGH (100%)** for 2 minutes. Stir in apple and microwave, uncovered, on **HIGH (100%)** for 1 minute or until sauce is thickened and apple is soft. Drain excess juice from liver; check doneness, then spoon sauce over liver. If liver is not done to your liking, microwave sauce-topped liver, uncovered, on **HIGH (100%)** for 1 to 2 more minutes.

Savory Chili

Preparation time: 10 minutes.
Microwaving time: 17 minutes.
Standing time: 3 minutes.

You can have this lightly spiced chili ready for the table in just 30 minutes—by using the microwave instead of a conventional range, you cut the cooking time by one full hour. Serve bowls of chili with tortilla chips and assorted raw vegetables.

- ½ **pound lean ground beef**
- 2 **tablespoons chopped onion**
- ½ **large green pepper, chopped**
- 1 **can (8 oz.) stewed tomatoes**
- 1 **can (8 oz.) tomato sauce**
- 2 **teaspoons chili powder**
- ½ **teaspoon ground cumin**

Crumble beef into a microwave-proof colander set in a medium-size microwave-proof bowl. Microwave, uncovered, on **HIGH (100%)** for 5 minutes; stir after 4 minutes, bringing uncooked meat to outside and pushing cooked meat to center. Drain off fat from bowl, then transfer cooked meat to bowl and add onion, green pepper, tomatoes (break up with a spoon), tomato sauce, chili powder, and cumin. Cover with heavy-duty plastic wrap and microwave on **HIGH (100%)** for 12 minutes, stirring after 6 minutes. Let stand for 3 minutes.

Orange-glazed Spareribs

Preparation time: 10 minutes.
Microwaving time: 42 minutes.
Standing time: 5 minutes.

Meaty pork ribs in an orange barbecue sauce make a finger-licking-good entrée. You'd need about 1½ hours to bake them in a conventional oven, but using the microwave on half power (50%), you'll have them ready in half that time. Serve corn on the cob and fresh fruit alongside; at meal's end, pass hot, lemon-scented towels (see Crab in Spicy Tomato Sauce, page 87).

- ¼ **cup frozen orange juice concentrate, thawed** (see page 90)
- 3 **tablespoons tomato-based chili sauce or catsup**
- 2 **tablespoons lemon juice**
- 1 **tablespoon brown sugar**
- 1½ **teaspoons Worcestershire**
- 1 **teaspoon prepared mustard**
- ¼ **to ½ teaspoon prepared horseradish**
- 2 **pounds spareribs, cut in serving-size pieces**

In a 1-cup glass measure, stir together orange juice concentrate, chili sauce, lemon juice, sugar, Worces-

tershire, mustard, and horseradish. Microwave, uncovered, on **HIGH (100%)** for 2 minutes; set aside.

Arrange ribs in a 7 by 11-inch microwave-proof dish, with large ends toward outside of dish. Cover with heavy-duty plastic wrap and microwave on **HIGH (100%)** for 10 minutes. Pour off accumulated juices. Turn ribs over; then bring uncooked center ribs to outside of dish and cooked ones to inside. Pour sauce over ribs. Cover with heavy-duty plastic wrap and microwave on **MEDIUM (50%)** for 20 minutes. Uncover. Turn ribs over and microwave, uncovered, on **MEDIUM (50%)** for 10 minutes. Let stand for 5 minutes. If ribs are not done to your liking, cover with heavy-duty plastic wrap and microwave on **MEDIUM (50%)** for 1 to 2 more minutes.

Pork Burgers

Preparation time: 10 minutes.
Microwaving time: 10 minutes.
Standing time: 3 minutes.

Cooked in a browning skillet, these moist pork patties look pan-fried. We suggest tucking them inside hamburger buns with lettuce and sliced tomatoes, but they're just as good topped with pineapple rings and served open-faced on English muffin halves. If you prefer beef to pork, try our taco burgers; they're delicious with fresh tomato salsa (page 93). Or serve them as cheeseburgers—just top patties with a few tablespoons of shredded Cheddar or jack cheese before letting them stand.

- ½ **pound lean ground pork**
- 1 **egg**
- 1 **clove garlic, minced or pressed**
- ½ **cup** *each* **finely chopped onion and chopped green pepper**
- ¼ **teaspoon** *each* **salt and ground cumin**
- ⅛ **teaspoon** *each* **pepper and oregano leaves**
- 2 **tablespoons fine dry bread crumbs**
- 1 **teaspoon salad oil**
- 2 **hamburger buns, split and toasted**
- 4 **thin slices tomato**
  Lettuce leaves

In a bowl, combine pork, egg, garlic, onion, green pepper, salt, cumin, pepper, oregano, and bread crumbs; blend well. Shape mixture into 2 patties, each about ½ inch thick.

Microwave a 10-inch browning dish or skillet on **HIGH (100%)** for 4½ minutes. Carefully transfer dish (bottom will be very hot) to a heatproof surface. Add oil and tilt dish to coat bottom evenly. Immediately place patties in dish; let stand until sizzling stops. Cover dish with lid or wax paper and microwave on **HIGH (100%)** for 3 minutes. Drain off fat. Turn patties over and microwave, uncovered, on **HIGH (100%)** for

2 minutes or until juices run clear when patties are slashed. Let stand, covered, for 3 minutes.

Drain patties briefly, then place on bottoms of buns and top each with 2 tomato slices and 1 or 2 lettuce leaves. Cover with tops of buns.

Taco Beef Burgers

Follow directions for **Pork Burgers,** but substitute ½ pound **lean ground beef** for pork, omit green pepper, and add ¾ teaspoon **chili powder,** 1 teaspoon **Worcestershire,** and 1 tablespoon **prepared taco sauce.**

Hot Wurst and Cabbage Salad

🕐 Preparation time: 12 minutes. Microwaving time: 9 minutes. Standing time: 1 minute

Dinner's a flash in the pan when you serve this hearty hot salad of crisp cabbage and sliced sausage in a tangy sweet-sour dressing. Choose red or green cabbage and your favorite fully cooked sausage; our test panel voted red cabbage and bockwurst the tastiest combination. Quick, simple accompaniments complete the meal: dinner rolls to go with the entrée, and ice cream sundaes for dessert.

  2 **tablespoons salad oil**
  ¾ **pound fully cooked sausages, such as bockwurst, kielbasa, knackwurst, or bratwurst, cut in ¼-inch-thick slices**
  4 **teaspoons white wine vinegar**
  1 **tablespoon sugar**
  1 **teaspoon** *each* **celery seed, Dijon mustard, and Worcestershire**
  1 **clove garlic, minced or pressed**
  ½ **cup thinly sliced green onions, including some tops**
  4 **cups finely shredded red or green cabbage Salt and pepper**

Microwave a 10-inch browning dish or skillet on **HIGH (100%)** for 4½ minutes. Carefully transfer dish (bottom will be very hot) to a heatproof surface. Add oil and tilt dish to coat bottom evenly. Immediately add sausages; stir and toss gently until sausages are lightly browned and sizzling stops. Microwave, uncovered, on **HIGH (100%)** for 1 minute. Transfer sausages to a dish and keep warm.

To drippings in browning dish, add vinegar, sugar, celery seed, mustard, Worcestershire, garlic, and onions; stir. Microwave, uncovered, on **HIGH (100%)** for 1 minute. Add cabbage; toss to coat with dressing. Microwave, uncovered, on **HIGH (100%)** for 2 minutes or just until wilted. Stir in sausages. Season to taste with salt and pepper. Let stand for 1 minute.

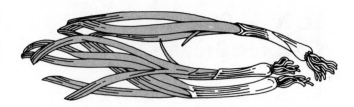

Minted Lamb Meatballs with Lemon Sauce

🕐 Preparation time: 15 minutes. Microwaving time: 8 minutes. Standing time: 3 minutes

Lamb—often seasoned with mint, lemon, and garlic—is a favorite throughout Greece. Here, tender meatballs flavored with mint and garlic are spooned over hot rice, then topped with a mildly tart lemon sauce. (Start the rice cooking before you mix up the meatballs.) Accompany with a salad of tomatoes and cucumbers; try refreshing Peppermint Tapioca Parfaits (page 76) for dessert.

  ½ **cup regular-strength chicken broth**
  1 **tablespoon lemon juice**
 1½ **teaspoons cornstarch**
  1 **egg**
  2 **teaspoons dry mint, crumbled**
  1 **large clove garlic, minced or pressed**
  1 **tablespoon all-purpose flour**
  ½ **teaspoon salt**
  ¼ **teaspoon pepper**
  ¾ **pound lean ground lamb**
  2 **tablespoons minced green onion, including some top**
  1 **tablespoon chopped parsley Hot cooked rice Lemon zest strips (optional)**

In a 1-cup glass measure, stir together broth, lemon juice, and cornstarch; set aside.

In a medium-size bowl, beat egg lightly. Add mint, garlic, flour, salt, pepper, and lamb; blend well. With dampened hands, shape lamb mixture into twelve 1½-inch meatballs. Place meatballs in a circle on a microwave-proof plate. Cover with wax paper and microwave on **HIGH (100%)** for 5 minutes. Drain off juices. Turn each meatball ¼ turn, re-cover, and microwave on **HIGH (100%)** for 1 more minute; let stand for 3 minutes.

While meatballs are standing, stir through broth mixture. Then microwave, uncovered, on **HIGH (100%)** for 2 minutes (stirring after 1 minute) or until bubbly and slightly thickened. Stir in onion and parsley. Let stand for 1 minute.

Spoon rice onto a platter. Arrange meatballs atop rice, then spoon sauce over meatballs. Garnish with lemon zest, if desired.

Teriyaki Ginger Chicken Breasts

🕐 *Preparation time: 11 minutes. Marinating time: 1 hour. Microwaving time: 5 minutes. Standing time: 3 minutes*

Boned, skinned chicken breasts absorb flavor in a gingery soy marinade, then microwave to moist and tender perfection. For a low-calorie meal, pair the chicken with stir-fried vegetables.

- 3 **tablespoons soy sauce**
- 1 **tablespoon e***ach* **sugar and dry sherry**
- ½ **teaspoon grated fresh ginger**
- 1 **clove garlic, minced or pressed**
- 1 **large whole chicken breast (1 to 1¼ lb.), split, boned, and skinned**
   Fresh cilantro (coriander) sprigs

In a 9-inch microwave-proof dish, stir together soy, sugar, sherry, ginger, and garlic. Add chicken and turn to coat with marinade. Cover and let marinate at room temperature for 1 hour, turning chicken over after 30 minutes.

Drain marinade from chicken and reserve. Cover dish with wax paper and microwave on **HIGH (100%)** for 3 minutes. Turn chicken over and brush with some of the marinade; re-cover and microwave on **HIGH (100%)** for 2 more minutes. Let stand for 3 minutes; chicken should no longer be pink when slashed in thickest part. Garnish with cilantro.

Swiss Chicken

🕐 *Preparation time: 15 minutes. Microwaving time: 6 minutes. Standing time: 5 minutes*

Boned chicken breasts in a creamy sauce are just right for an elegant dinner à *deux*. Round out the menu with a green salad and buttered noodles or rice.

- 1 **large whole chicken breast (1 to 1¼ lb.), split, boned, and skinned**
- ¼ **teaspoon e***ach* **salt and paprika**
- 1 **teaspoon cornstarch**
- 2 **tablespoons cream sherry**
- ⅓ **cup whipping cream**
- ½ **cup shredded Swiss cheese**
   Chopped parsley

Place chicken, skinned side up, in a 1-quart microwave-proof dish. In a small bowl, combine salt, paprika, and cornstarch; stir in sherry and cream, blend well, and pour over chicken. Cover dish with lid or heavy-duty plastic wrap. Microwave on **MEDIUM-HIGH (70%)** for 4 minutes, stirring sauce after 2 minutes and spooning it over chicken.

Rotate each piece of chicken ½ turn; spoon sauce over chicken. Cover with lid or heavy-duty plastic wrap; microwave on **MEDIUM-HIGH (70%)** for 1 minute. Sprinkle chicken with cheese and parsley. Microwave, uncovered, on **HIGH (100%)** for 30 seconds or until cheese is melted. Let stand for 5 minutes; chicken should no longer be pink when slashed in thickest part.

Sweet Chili Chicken

🕐 *Preparation time: 10 minutes. Microwaving time: 14 minutes. Standing time: 5 minutes*

For a low-calorie entrée, try tender dark-meat chicken coated with a tangy, slightly sweet chili sauce. Traditional barbecue accompaniments—corn on the cob and coleslaw—taste delicious alongside.

- ½ **cup tomato-based chili sauce**
- 1 **tablespoon e***ach* **white (distilled) vinegar, brown sugar, and minced green onion**
- ½ **teaspoon e***ach* **dry mustard and Worcestershire**
- 2 **chicken legs with thighs attached (about 1¼ lb. total), skinned**

In a 9-inch microwave-proof dish, stir together chili sauce, vinegar, sugar, onion, mustard, and Worcestershire. Add chicken and turn to coat, then arrange with thighs toward outside of dish. Cover with heavy-duty plastic wrap and microwave on **HIGH (100%)** for 7 minutes. Turn pieces over so uncooked portions are toward outside of dish; spoon sauce over top, cover with heavy-duty plastic wrap, and microwave on **HIGH (100%)** for 5 minutes. Then uncover and microwave on **HIGH (100%)** for 2 more minutes or until sauce is thickened. Let stand for 5 minutes; meat near thigh-bone should no longer be pink when slashed.

Italian-style Chicken Scallops

Preparation time: 15 minutes. Microwaving time: 10 minutes.
Standing time: 3 minutes

The microwave browning dish works its magic to give these pounded chicken breasts their golden, pan-fried appearance. For best browning, microwave the browning dish until it's very hot; pour in oil, add chicken scallops, and let stand until sizzling stops. Then turn scallops over and complete the cooking. Serve microwaved green beans (page 85) alongside. Or, for a more elegant side dish, offer Spinach Soufflé-stuffed Mushrooms (page 65)—slip them into the oven as soon as you start to heat the browning dish. (See photograph on page 78.)

1 **large whole chicken breast (1 to 1¼ lb.), split, boned, and skinned**
2 **tablespoons e*ach* fine dry bread crumbs, all-purpose flour, and grated Parmesan cheese**
½ **teaspoon Italian herb seasoning or ¼ teaspoon e*ach* oregano leaves and dry basil**
⅛ **teaspoon e*ach* pepper and ground coriander**
1 **egg**
1½ **tablespoons olive oil or salad oil**
1 **can (about 8 oz.) marinara sauce**
⅓ **cup shredded mozzarella cheese**

Place chicken breast halves, one at a time, between 2 sheets of plastic wrap. With flat side of a mallet, gently pound meat until about ⅜ inch thick; set aside.

In a rimmed plate, stir together bread crumbs, flour, Parmesan cheese, herb seasoning, pepper, and coriander. In another rimmed plate, beat egg until blended. Dip each chicken piece into egg to coat, then dredge in crumb mixture until coated. Place coated chicken piece on a flat surface and press crumb mixture into meat with your fingers.

Microwave a 10-inch browning dish or skillet on **HIGH (100%)** for 4½ minutes. Carefully transfer dish (bottom will be very hot) to a heatproof surface. Add oil and tilt dish to coat bottom evenly. At once place chicken pieces in dish, in a single layer. Slightly tilt dish so oil touches each piece; then let stand until sizzling stops. Turn pieces over and microwave, uncovered, on **HIGH (100%)** for 2 minutes. Rotate each piece ½ turn. Evenly top each with about 3 tablespoons of the marinara sauce (reserve remaining sauce) and microwave, uncovered, on **HIGH (100%)** for 1½ minutes. Evenly sprinkle mozzarella cheese over chicken and microwave, uncovered, on **HIGH (100%)** for 30 seconds. Let stand for 3 minutes.

Meanwhile, place reserved sauce in a small microwave-proof serving bowl and microwave, uncovered, on **HIGH (100%)** for 1 minute or until heated through. Pass at the table to spoon over chicken.

Indian Chicken Curry

Preparation time: 10 minutes. Microwaving time: 19 minutes.
Standing time: 3 minutes

Serve up an Indian feast tonight, starring chicken legs and thighs in a fragrant, mild-tasting curry sauce. The sauce is laced with onion and bits of apple—and there's plenty of it, so be sure to offer lots of hot rice with the chicken. By cooking the curry in the microwave, you can have everything ready to serve in just half an hour. Prepare the condiments first, then start the rice right before you begin microwaving the curry. Complete the main course with broiled tomato halves; you can pop them under the broiler while the chicken is standing.

Condiments (suggestions follow)
3 **tablespoons butter or margarine**
½ **cup e*ach* chopped onion and finely chopped Golden Delicious apple**
2 **tablespoons all-purpose flour**
2½ **teaspoons curry powder**
¼ **teaspoon ground ginger**
1 **teaspoon sugar**
½ **cup e*ach* milk and regular-strength chicken broth**
1 **teaspoon lemon juice**
2 **chicken legs with thighs attached (about 1¼ lb. total)**
Hot cooked rice

Prepare condiments of your choice and place in individual bowls; set aside.

Place butter in a 9-inch microwave-proof dish. Microwave, uncovered, on **HIGH (100%)** for 1 minute or until melted. Stir in onion and apple. Microwave, uncovered, on **HIGH (100%)** for 3 minutes or until soft. Stir in flour, curry powder, ginger, and sugar. Microwave, uncovered, on **HIGH (100%)** for 1 minute or until bubbly. Stirring constantly, gradually stir in milk and broth; blend well, then stir in lemon juice.

Add chicken to dish and turn to coat all sides. Arrange chicken with thighs toward outside of dish. Cover with heavy-duty plastic wrap and microwave on **HIGH (100%)** for 7 minutes. Turn pieces over so uncooked portions are toward outside of dish; spoon sauce over top, cover with heavy-duty plastic wrap, and microwave on **HIGH (100%)** for 7 more minutes. Let stand for 3 minutes; meat near thighbone should no longer be pink when slashed.

To serve, mound rice on 2 dinner plates. Top each mound with a piece of chicken; spoon sauce over chicken and rice. Pass condiments at the table.

Condiments. Use **salted peanuts**, shredded **coconut**, diced **avocado**, **raisins**, sliced **green onion**, sliced **banana**, chopped **hard-cooked egg**, **sweet pickle chips**, or **chutney**.

Chicken Livers with Bacon and Onions

⏱ *Preparation time: 15 minutes. Microwaving time: 20 minutes. Standing time: 3 minutes*

Crisp bacon and a hint of rosemary flavor this classic chicken liver dish, simplified by microwave cooking. To keep your oven clean, be sure to cover the livers with wax paper—they tend to spatter when microwaved. And be careful not to overcook; when you take the dish from the oven, livers should still be very pink inside (they'll continue to cook as they stand).

- 2 **tablespoons all-purpose flour**
- ¼ **teaspoon e*ach* salt and pepper**
- ¼ **teaspoon dry rosemary, crumbled**
- ¾ **pound chicken livers, cut in half and drained**
- 4 **slices bacon**
- 1 **small onion, thinly sliced and separated into rings**
- 1 **tablespoon Madeira or dry sherry**
  Chopped parsley

In a rimmed plate, stir together flour, salt, pepper, and rosemary. Dredge chicken livers in flour mixture and set aside.

Place bacon, in a single layer, on a microwave-proof rack over a microwave-proof dish. Cover with a paper towel and microwave on **HIGH (100%)** for 5 minutes or until slices look crisp (they'll become crisper on standing). Place bacon on another paper towel and let drain. Pour off and reserve all but 1 tablespoon drippings. Add onion to drippings remaining in dish; stir to coat. Microwave, uncovered, on **HIGH (100%)** for 6 minutes (stirring after 4 minutes) or until soft; set aside.

Microwave a 10-inch browning dish or skillet on **HIGH (100%)** for 4½ minutes. Carefully transfer dish (bottom will be very hot) to a heatproof surface. Add 1½ tablespoons of the reserved drippings and tilt dish to coat bottom evenly. Immediately place chicken liver pieces, sides not touching, in hot drippings. Slightly tilt dish so drippings touch each liver piece; then let stand until sizzling stops.

Turn livers over; bring any pieces that look raw to outside of dish. Sprinkle with Madeira. Cover with lid

or wax paper and microwave on **HIGH (100%)** for 2 minutes. Bring any pieces that still look raw to outside of dish and push cooked ones to inside; sprinkle onion over livers. Cover with lid or wax paper and microwave on **HIGH (100%)** for 2 minutes (all livers should be very pink when slashed). Let stand for 3 minutes. Crumble bacon over livers, then sprinkle with parsley.

Hot Chicken Salad in Tomato Cups

⏱ *Preparation time: 35 minutes. Microwaving time: 7 minutes. Standing time: 3 minutes*

Whole tomatoes cut to resemble flowers make perfect edible containers for individual servings of hot chicken and artichoke salad. You can use the creamy chicken mixture for knife-and-fork open-faced sandwiches, too—just spoon it over toasted English muffins.

- 1 **whole chicken breast (about 1 lb.), split, boned, and skinned**
- 2 **large beefsteak tomatoes, peeled if desired**
  Lettuce leaves
- ⅓ **cup chopped green onions, including some tops**
- ⅓ **cup chopped celery**
- 1 **jar (6 oz.) marinated artichoke hearts, drained well and chopped**
- 1 **jar (2 oz.) sliced pimentos, drained well**
- ½ **cup shredded Cheddar cheese**
- 3 **tablespoons mayonnaise**
  Salt and pepper
  Chopped parsley

Place chicken breast halves on a microwave-proof plate. Cover with wax paper and microwave on **HIGH (100%)** for 4 minutes. Let stand for 3 minutes; chicken should no longer be pink when slashed in thickest part. Drain off and discard juices, then cover chicken loosely and refrigerate until cooled (about 30 minutes).

Meanwhile, cut stems out of tomatoes. Then, without cutting all the way through, cut each tomato in 6 to 8 wedges. Line 2 salad plates with lettuce leaves and place a tomato on each. Carefully spread tomatoes open to resemble flowers; set aside.

In a 2-quart microwave-proof bowl, combine onions, celery, artichokes, pimentos (reserve a few slices for garnish), cheese, and mayonnaise. Cut chicken in bite-size chunks and add to bowl. Stir just until mayonnaise and cheese are distributed throughout; then season mixture to taste with salt and pepper.

Cover bowl with wax paper and microwave on **MEDIUM (50%)** for 3 minutes (stirring after 1½ minutes) or until heated through. Mound chicken mixture equally in center of tomatoes; garnish with reserved pimento slices and parsley.

Cooking Fresh Vegetables in the Microwave

All vegetables are cooked on **HIGH (100%).** For even cooking, cut vegetables in uniform pieces. Exact cooking time depends on maturity and moisture content of vegetables; start with the shortest time, then allow to stand for recommended time before microwaving further, in 30-second increments. Unless otherwise noted, cooked vegetables should be tender-crisp.

VEGETABLE & AMOUNT	CONTAINER	SELECTION & PREPARATION	COOKING TIME (CT) STANDING TIME (ST)
ARTICHOKES 2 medium (6–8 oz. *each*)	9" round microwave-proof dish	Remove coarse outer leaves. Trim stems so artichokes will stand upright. Cut off top ⅓ of artichokes; trim thorn from tip of each leaf. Rinse artichokes and turn upside down in dish. Add ½ cup water. Cover with heavy-duty plastic wrap.	CT: 8–10 minutes Before standing, lower leaves should pull away from stem with just a slight tug; stem should be tender when pierced. ST: 5 minutes, covered
ASPARAGUS 1 bunch (1 lb.)	7x11" microwave-proof dish	Snap off tough ends; rinse. Arrange asparagus spears in dish with buds toward center and stalk ends toward outside. Add 3 tablespoons water. Cover with heavy-duty plastic wrap.	CT: 5 minutes Rearrange spears halfway through cooking, bringing center pieces to edge of dish; re-cover. ST: 5 minutes, covered
BEANS, GREEN OR WAX ½ lb.	1-qt. microwave-proof casserole	Snap off both ends of beans and pull off strings. Rinse beans and cut in 1" pieces. Place in dish and add ¼ cup water. Cover with lid or heavy-duty plastic wrap.	CT: 6–7 minutes Stir after 4 minutes; re-cover. ST: 5 minutes, covered Degree of tenderness depends on maturity of beans and variety used.
BROCCOLI 1 small bunch (⅔–1 lb.)	7x11" microwave-proof dish or flat 12" microwave-proof plate	Cut bunch in uniform spears, leaving about 3½" of stalk on each spear. Peel skin off bottom 2" of stalks. Rinse broccoli and arrange in dish with flowerets toward center and stalk ends toward outside. *Do not add water.* Cover with heavy-duty plastic wrap.	CT: 4–5 minutes If using 7x11" dish, rearrange spears halfway through cooking, bringing center pieces to edge of dish; re-cover. If using plate, just rotate plate ¼ turn. ST: 4 minutes, covered
CARROTS ½ lb.	1-qt. microwave-proof casserole	Select carrots about 1" in diameter. Scrub well or peel with a vegetable peeler; cut off ends, then cut carrots in ¼"-thick slices. Place in dish and add 1 tablespoon water. Cover with lid or heavy-duty plastic wrap.	CT: 4–5 minutes Stir after 3 minutes; re-cover. ST: 5 minutes, covered
CORN 2 ears	None	Be sure corn is completely enclosed in husk; secure ends with string or rubber bands. (Or remove husk and silk and wrap each ear individually in heavy-duty plastic wrap. Arrange on paper towels on oven floor, placing ears side by side and at least 1" apart.	CT: 6–8 minutes Turn each ear over halfway through cooking. ST: 2–3 minutes
POTATOES, RUSSET 2 potatoes (about 8 oz. *each*)	None	Scrub potatoes well, then pierce skin on all 4 sides with fork or knife. Arrange on paper towels on oven floor, placing potatoes side by side and at least 1" apart.	CT: 6–8 minutes Turn each potato over halfway through cooking. After cooking, potatoes should give slightly when squeezed. For standing, wrap potatoes in a clean towel or in foil. ST: 5–10 minutes, covered
POTATOES, SWEET (OR YAMS) 2 potatoes (about 8 oz. *each*)	None	Choose fairly round sweet potatoes. Prepare and arrange as for russet potatoes (above).	CT: 6–7 minutes Follow directions given for russet potatoes. ST: 5–10 minutes, covered
SPINACH ⅔–¾ lb.	2-qt. microwave-proof casserole	Rinse leaves well and shake off excess moisture. Place in dish; *do not add water.* Cover with lid or heavy-duty plastic wrap.	CT: 3–5 minutes Stir after 1 minute; re-cover. ST: 2 minutes, covered
SQUASH, SUMMER CROOKNECK, PATTYPAN, or ZUCCHINI ½ lb.	1-qt. microwave-proof casserole	Remove ends; rinse squash and cut in ¼"-thick slices. Place in dish; add 1 tablespoon water (or 1 tablespoon butter or margarine, cut in pieces). Cover with lid or heavy-duty plastic wrap.	CT: 3–4 minutes Stir after 3 minutes; re-cover. ST: 3 minutes, covered

Game Hens with Apricots

⏱ *Thaw frozen birds. Preparation time: 10 minutes. Microwaving time: 19 to 20 minutes. Standing time: 5 minutes*

A special occasion calls for a special dinner. What better way to celebrate than with these elegant apricot-sauced game hens? Accompany with microwaved green beans (page 85), then finish the meal with Meringue Heart Sundaes (page 76). Don't forget the champagne and candlelight!

  2 **Rock Cornish game hens (20 to 24 oz. each)**
  2 **tablespoons each bottled brown gravy sauce and water, stirred together**
  ½ **cup apricot preserves**
  ¼ **teaspoon prepared mustard**
  1 **tablespoon dry sherry**
  1 **teaspoon lemon juice**
  1 **pound apricots, halved, pitted, and sprinkled with lemon juice; or 1 can (1 lb.) apricot halves, drained well**
     Watercress (optional)

Thaw hens as directed on package (set giblets aside for other uses); rinse hens and pat completely dry. Brush hens with about half the gravy mixture; then place, breast side down, on a microwave-proof rack in a 7 by 11-inch microwave-proof dish. Cover with wax paper and microwave on **HIGH (100%)** for 6 minutes. Turn hens over and brush with remaining gravy mixture. Cover with wax paper and microwave on **HIGH (100%)** for 6 more minutes.

Meanwhile prepare apricot glaze: in a microwave-proof bowl, stir together preserves, mustard, sherry, and lemon juice. Brush hens with some of the glaze. Microwave, uncovered, on **HIGH (100%)** for 3 minutes. Turn birds over and brush with more apricot glaze. Microwave, uncovered, on **HIGH (100%)** for 3 more minutes. Cover very loosely with foil and let stand for 5 minutes; meat near thighbone should no longer be pink when slashed.

Gently stir apricot halves into remaining apricot glaze. Microwave, uncovered, on **HIGH (100%)** for 1 to 2 minutes or until heated through. Arrange glazed apricots around hens. Garnish with watercress, if desired.

Lemon-Soy Turkey Legs

⏱ *Preparation time: 10 minutes. Marinating time: 8 to 24 hours. Microwaving time: 54 minutes. Standing time: 15 minutes*

A flavorful lemon-soy mixture does double duty in this entrée—it's both marinade and sauce for turkey drumsticks. Steamed brown rice and buttered microwaved broccoli spears (page 85) make excellent accompaniments.

  ¼ **cup each soy sauce and water**
  2 **tablespoons each dry sherry and lemon juice**
  1 **tablespoon sugar**
  2 **teaspoons finely minced fresh ginger**
  2 **cloves garlic, minced or pressed**
  ½ **teaspoon grated lemon peel**
     Dash of pepper
  2 **large turkey legs (about 1¼ lb. each)**
  2 **tablespoons cornstarch**
  ⅓ **cup regular-strength chicken broth**

In a 7 by 11-inch microwave-proof dish, stir together soy, water, sherry, lemon juice, sugar, ginger, garlic, lemon peel, and pepper. Add turkey legs and turn to coat on all sides with marinade. Cover and refrigerate for at least 8 hours or up to 24 hours, turning legs over 2 or 3 times.

Drain marinade into a 2-cup glass measure and set aside. Arrange turkey legs so large ends are toward outside of dish, then cover with heavy-duty plastic wrap and microwave on **HIGH (100%)** for 10 minutes. Turn legs over. Microwave, uncovered, on **MEDIUM-LOW (30%)** for 40 minutes, turning legs over after 20 minutes. Cover and let stand for 15 minutes; meat near bone should no longer be pink when slashed. If meat is not done to your liking, cover dish with heavy-duty plastic wrap and microwave on **MEDIUM-LOW (30%)** for 4 to 8 more minutes; check for doneness after 4 minutes.

Microwave reserved marinade, uncovered, on **HIGH (100%)** for 2 minutes or until boiling. Stir together cornstarch and broth; add to marinade and microwave, uncovered, on **HIGH (100%)** for 2 minutes (stirring after 1 minute) or until sauce is thickened. Pass at the table to spoon over individual servings. If you have leftover turkey and sauce, refrigerate them separately.

Clams with Garlic Butter

⏱ *Preparation time: 10 minutes. Microwaving time: 4 to 6 minutes. Standing time: 1 minute*

It's fun to watch clams steaming in the microwave—they pop open in just a few minutes. Serve the cooked clams in their shells, drizzled with garlic butter, and offer plenty of French bread to catch the drips. Follow the entrée with a crisp green salad and a dessert of fresh fruit and cheese.

- ¼ **cup butter or margarine**
- 1 **small clove garlic, minced or pressed**
- 1 **tablespoon chopped parsley**
- ¼ **teaspoon lemon juice**
- 1 **dozen fresh clams or mussels in the shell, well scrubbed**

Place butter, garlic, parsley, and lemon juice in a small microwave-proof serving bowl. Microwave, uncovered, on **HIGH (100%)** for 1 minute or until butter is melted; set aside.

Arrange clams in a circle on a flat 10-inch microwave-proof plate. Cover loosely with heavy-duty plastic wrap, leaving enough room for shells to open. Microwave on **HIGH (100%)** for 3 to 5 minutes or until shells pop open. If any clams remain unopened, lift out opened clams; then microwave unopened ones on **HIGH (100%)** until shells open, checking at 30-second intervals. Let stand for 1 minute. Serve in shells, drizzled with garlic butter.

Pesto Shrimp Pasta

⏱ *Preparation time: 15 minutes. Microwaving time: 6 minutes. Standing time: 2 minutes*

If you like shrimp, garlic, and basil, you'll love this pasta with pesto sauce and shrimp. Watch the shrimp closely as they cook—as soon as those near outside of dish turn pink, push them to the inside. (If overcooked, they'll become rubbery.) Complete the meal with a tomato and cucumber salad, bread sticks, and chilled wine.

- 6 **ounces spaghetti or fettuccine**
- 1 **cup lightly packed fresh basil leaves (or 1 cup finely chopped parsley and 2 teaspoons dry basil)**
- ⅓ **cup grated Parmesan cheese**
- 4 **cloves garlic**
- 3 **tablespoons lemon juice**
- 4 **tablespoons olive oil**
- 3 **tablespoons butter or margarine**
- ¾ **pound medium-size raw shrimp, shelled and deveined**
  Zest of 1 lemon, cut in thin strips

Following package directions, cook pasta in a large kettle of boiling salted water until *al dente*. While pasta cooks, place basil, cheese, 1 clove of the garlic (cut in pieces), lemon juice, and 3 tablespoons of the oil in a food processor or blender; whirl until puréed. Set aside.

Mince or press remaining 3 cloves garlic; place in a 1½-quart microwave-proof dish and add remaining 1 tablespoon oil and 2 tablespoons of the butter. Microwave, uncovered, on **HIGH (100%)** for 2 minutes or until garlic is soft. Stir in shrimp. Microwave, uncovered, on **HIGH (100%)** for 4 minutes or until all shrimp are pink (stir after 2 minutes to bring cooked shrimp to inside of dish). Stir in pesto sauce, cover, and let stand for 2 minutes.

Drain pasta well; toss with remaining 1 tablespoon butter and mound on a platter. Spoon shrimp and pesto mixture over pasta and toss lightly to coat pasta strands. Sprinkle with lemon zest.

Crab in Spicy Tomato Sauce

⏱ *Preparation time: 10 minutes. Microwaving time: 4 minutes. Standing time: None required*

Messy, but so delicious—that describes this entrée. You cook crab pieces in the shell in a zesty tomato sauce, then spoon into bowls to eat out of hand. Serve other finger foods alongside—crusty bread or rolls and a selection of relishes.

When the last shell is emptied, offer your guests hot, lemon-scented towels from the microwave. Before you begin to eat, dampen towels and wring out excess moisture; then sprinkle towels lightly with lemon juice, roll them up, and set on the microwave floor. To heat towels, just microwave on **HIGH (100%)** for 1 to 2 minutes.

- 1 **cup catsup**
- ½ **cup hot water**
- 2 **whole cloves**
- ½ **teaspoon seasoned salt**
- ¼ **teaspoon e*ach* thyme leaves and sugar**
- 1½ **teaspoons Worcestershire**
- ½ **teaspoon prepared horseradish**
- 1 **bay leaf**
- 1 **large cooked Dungeness crab (about 2 lb.), cleaned and cracked**

In a 1½ to 2-quart microwave-proof dish, stir together catsup, water, cloves, salt, thyme, sugar, Worcestershire, horseradish, and bay leaf. Microwave, uncovered, on **HIGH (100%)** for 2 minutes (stirring after 1 minute) or until bubbly. Add crab pieces. Microwave, uncovered, on **HIGH (100%)** for 2 minutes or until heated through. Spoon into individual bowls.

Scallops with Pea Pods

 Preparation time: 15 minutes. Marinating time: 30 minutes. Microwaving time: 6 minutes. Standing time: 4 minutes

Scallops and fresh shiitake mushrooms are marinated in teriyaki sauce, then briefly cooked and served over bright green edible-pod peas (often called Chinese pea pods). Steamed rice and hot jasmine tea are suitable accompaniments. If you can't find fresh shiitake mushrooms, use 1 ounce Oriental dried mushrooms. Soak them in warm water to cover for 30 minutes; cut off and discard stems, then thinly slice caps.

- **1 green onion, including some top**
- **3 ounces fresh shiitake mushrooms, cut in thin strips**
- **¾ pound scallops, rinsed and cut in bite-size pieces**
- **3 quarter-size slices fresh ginger**
- **5 teaspoons salad oil**
- **4 teaspoons soy sauce**
- **2 teaspoons dry sherry**
- **½ pound edible-pod peas, ends and strings removed, rinsed well but not patted dry**

Cut onion lengthwise in thin strips, then crosswise in 1-inch pieces. Reserve some of the onion slivers for garnish; place remainder in a shallow 1½-quart microwave-proof dish and add mushrooms, scallops, and ginger. Stir together oil, soy, and sherry until blended; pour over scallops and let marinate at room temperature for 30 minutes, stirring after 15 minutes.

Spread scallops out in a single layer. Cover with wax paper and microwave on **HIGH (100%)** for 3 minutes (stirring after 2 minutes) or until scallops are opaque throughout. Let stand for 4 minutes.

Meanwhile, place peas (with water that clings to them) in a 1-quart microwave-proof dish. Cover with lid or heavy-duty plastic wrap and microwave on **HIGH (100%)** for 3 minutes (stirring after 2 minutes). Let stand for 1 minute, then place in a serving dish. Remove and discard ginger from scallop mixture; spoon scallop mixture over peas. Garnish with reserved onion slivers.

Oyster Stew

 Preparation time: 15 minutes. Microwaving time: 19 minutes. Standing time: 3 minutes

Potatoes, onions, and oysters in a creamy broth make a light but filling entrée. If you wish, you can use monkfish in place of oysters; it's lean and firm-textured, with a flavor reminiscent of lobster. You can cook oysters or fish to succulent perfection without microwaving—just stir into bubbling broth and let steep until done.

- **3 tablespoons butter or margarine**
- **1 small onion, chopped**
- **½ cup finely chopped celery**
- **½ cup finely chopped parsley**
- **1 medium-size thin-skinned potato (peeled if desired), cut in ½-inch cubes**
- **1 can (14½ oz.) regular-strength chicken broth**
- **½ pint (1 cup) whipping cream**
- **¾ teaspoon white pepper**
- **½ teaspoon salt**
- **1 tablespoon cornstarch mixed with 2 tablespoons water**
- **1 jar (10 oz.) oysters, cut in pieces (reserve liquid); or ½ pound monkfish, membrane removed, cut in ¾-inch pieces**

Place 2 tablespoons of the butter in a 2-quart microwave-proof dish. Microwave, uncovered, on **HIGH (100%)** for 30 seconds or until melted. Stir in onion, celery, ⅓ cup of the parsley, and potato. Cover with lid or heavy-duty plastic wrap and microwave on **HIGH (100%)** for 10 minutes (stirring after 5 minutes) or just until potato is tender when pierced.

Stir in broth, cream, pepper, salt, and cornstarch mixture. Microwave, uncovered, on **HIGH (100%)** for 8 minutes (stirring after 5 minutes) or until broth is bubbly and slightly thickened. Stir in oysters and their liquid. Cover and let stand for 3 minutes. If oysters aren't done to your liking, let them steep for a few more minutes. Place remaining 1 tablespoon butter in center of stew and sprinkle with remaining parsley.

Fisherman's Chowder

⏱ Preparation time: 15 minutes. Microwaving time: 16 minutes. Standing time: 3 minutes

A quick, sturdy soup to satisfy hearty appetites, this tomato-based chowder is thick with white fish, shrimp, vegetables, and bacon. A crisp spinach salad and crusty rolls round out the meal.

  2 slices bacon, cut in 1-inch pieces
  1 small onion, chopped
  2 cloves garlic, minced or pressed
  1 can (about 15 oz.) pear-shaped tomatoes
  ¼ cup dry vermouth
  1 teaspoon Worcestershire
  2 bay leaves
  ¼ teaspoon pepper
  ½ pound fish fillets (lingcod, red snapper, perch, or swordfish), *each* about ¾ inch thick, cut in ¾-inch pieces
  ¼ pound small cooked shrimp
     Salt
     Chopped parsley

Place bacon in a 3-quart microwave-proof dish, separating pieces with a fork. Cover with wax paper and microwave on **HIGH (100%)** for 4 minutes, stirring after 3 minutes. With a slotted spoon, lift out bacon and place on paper towels to drain. Pour off and discard all but 2 tablespoons drippings.

Add onion and garlic to drippings in dish. Microwave, uncovered, on **HIGH (100%)** for 4 minutes. Add tomatoes (break up with a spoon) and their liquid, vermouth, Worcestershire, bay leaves, and pepper. Cover with lid or wax paper and microwave on **HIGH (100%)** for 6 minutes (stirring after 4 minutes) or until hot and bubbly. Stir in fish and microwave, uncovered, on **HIGH (100%)** for 2 minutes.

Stir in shrimp and bacon. Cover and let stand for 3 minutes; fish should flake readily when prodded with a fork. Season to taste with salt. Remove and discard bay leaves; sprinkle chowder with parsley.

Shark Steaks with Mushrooms

⏱ Preparation time: 10 minutes. Marinating time: 30 to 60 minutes. Microwaving time: 8 minutes. Standing time: 3 minutes

Fish markets around the country sell a number of different varieties of shark—leopard, thresher, dogfish, and grayfish, to name just four. All are boneless and mild-flavored, with a firm, moist, meaty texture. Here, a lemon marinade flavors thick shark steaks topped with mushrooms (if you can't find shark, substitute swordfish).

  2 tablespoons *each* lemon juice and dry white wine
  1 clove garlic, minced or pressed
  ¼ teaspoon *each* oregano leaves and salt
  ¼ teaspoon fennel seed, crushed
  ⅛ teaspoon pepper
  1 tablespoon olive oil or salad oil
  2 shark steaks (¾ to 1 lb. total), *each* about 1 inch thick
  ¼ pound mushrooms, thinly sliced
     Chopped chives

In a 9-inch microwave-proof dish, stir together lemon juice, wine, garlic, oregano, salt, fennel seed, pepper, and oil. Add fish and turn several times to coat well. Let marinate at room temperature for 30 to 60 minutes, turning every 15 minutes. Drain marinade into a microwave-proof bowl and stir in mushrooms.

Arrange fish with thickest portions toward outside of dish; cover with wax paper. Microwave on **HIGH (100%)** for 5 minutes, rotating each steak ½ turn after 3 minutes. Let stand for 3 minutes; fish should flake readily when prodded in thickest portion with a fork.

While fish stands, microwave mushroom mixture, uncovered, on **HIGH (100%)** for 3 minutes, stirring after 2 minutes. Transfer fish to a serving plate; top with mushroom mixture. Sprinkle with chives.

Microwave Tips

Microwave cooking is even faster when you know a few tricks like these.

Softening cream cheese. Unwrap one small package (3 oz.) cream cheese; place on a microwave-proof plate. Cover with wax paper and microwave on **MEDIUM (50%)** for 30 seconds; let stand for 2 minutes.

Thawing frozen juice concentrate. Remove one end of one small can (6 oz.) frozen orange juice concentrate. Place, upright, on oven floor. Microwave, uncovered, on **HIGH (100%)** for 30 seconds; let stand for 2 minutes.

Getting more juice from lemons. Place a lemon on oven floor. Microwave on **HIGH (100%)** for 15 seconds. Roll fruit between palms; then cut and squeeze out juice.

Vegetable-topped Poached Fish

 Preparation time: 11 minutes. Microwaving time: 15 minutes. Standing time: 9 to 13 minutes

Forgot to defrost something for dinner tonight? Don't fret—with the microwave's help, frozen fish fillets go from freezer to table in just 35 minutes. Each fillet is crowned with a creamy vegetable topping, then embellished with tomato wedges.

Be sure fish is fully thawed before cooking, even if that means letting it stand a bit longer.

> 2 **tablespoons butter or margarine**
> ½ **cup finely grated carrot**
> 3 **tablespoons chopped green onions, including some tops**
> 2 **tablespoons lemon juice**
> 1 **small package (3 oz.) cream cheese, softened (see above)**
> 1 **tablespoon minced parsley**
> ¼ **teaspoon white pepper**
> 1 **package (12 oz.) frozen fish fillets (sole, cod, perch, or haddock)**
> **Thin tomato wedges**

Place butter in a small microwave-proof bowl. Microwave, uncovered, on **HIGH (100%)** for 30 seconds or until melted. Stir in carrot and onions. Microwave,

uncovered, on **HIGH (100%)** for 4 minutes or until vegetables are soft. Let cool slightly; then add lemon juice, cream cheese, parsley, and pepper. Blend well and set aside.

Stack 2 paper towels on oven floor. Place unopened fish package on towels and microwave on **MEDIUM (50%)** for 5 minutes, turning package over after 2 minutes. Open package and let stand for 6 to 10 minutes or until fish is thawed. If fish is still frozen in center, cover package with paper towels and microwave on **MEDIUM (50%)** for 1 more minute, then let stand until thawed.

Separate fish into fillets and pat dry; then place in a 9-inch microwave-proof dish, with thickest portions toward outside of dish. Cover with lid or heavy-duty plastic wrap and microwave on **HIGH (100%)** for 3 minutes. Rotate each fillet ½ turn, then spread cheese-vegetable mixture evenly over each. Microwave, uncovered, on **MEDIUM-HIGH (70%)** for 2 minutes. Let stand for 3 minutes; fish should flake readily when prodded in thickest portion with a fork. Top each fillet with a few tomato wedges.

Halibut Pil-pil

 Preparation time: 10 minutes. Microwaving time: 10 minutes. Standing time: 3 minutes

Here's a microwave adaptation of a Basque classic. You poach fish steaks in seasoned olive oil, then purée the oil with cooked bell pepper to make a delicate sauce with the texture of a thin mayonnaise. The pepper both thickens the sauce and gives it its vivid color. Serve *pil-pil* hot, at room temperature, or chilled, with asparagus and tiny new potatoes. (It's spicy and rich, so follow it with a simple dessert.)

> 1 **tablespoon dry white wine**
> 2 **tablespoons lemon juice**
> ¼ **to ½ teaspoon crushed dried hot red chiles**
> 6 **tablespoons olive oil**
> 2 **cloves garlic, halved**
> 1 **small red bell pepper, seeded and cut in thin strips; or ½ cup canned roasted red peppers (any charred skins removed), drained and patted dry**
> 2 **halibut or lingcod steaks (¾ to 1 lb. total),** *each* **about ¾ inch thick**
> **Salt**

In a small dish, stir together wine, lemon juice, and chiles; set aside. Pour oil into a 9-inch microwave-proof dish. Add garlic and bell pepper. Microwave, uncovered, on **HIGH (100%)** for 6 minutes (stirring after 3 minutes) or until vegetables are soft. Discard garlic; lift out pepper strips, place on paper towels, and let drain.

Cut fish steaks in half lengthwise and pat dry; then place in hot oil, with thickest portions toward outside of dish. Cover with wax paper and microwave on **HIGH (100%)** for 2 minutes. Blend wine mixture into oil in dish. Turn fish over so uncooked portions are toward outside of dish; re-cover and microwave on **MEDIUM-HIGH (70%)** for 2 minutes. Let stand for 3 minutes; fish should flake readily when prodded in thickest portion with a fork.

With a wide spatula, carefully transfer fish to a hot serving dish; keep warm. Pour oil mixture into a blender or food processor; add pepper strips and any fish juices that have collected on serving dish. Whirl until puréed and slightly thickened. Season sauce to taste with salt and pour over fish; serve hot. Or let fish and sauce cool (separately) to room temperature, then serve; or cover and refrigerate cooled sauce and fish separately for up to 24 hours and serve cold.

Garlic-Lemon Red Snapper

 Preparation time: 7 minutes. Microwaving time: 13 to 15 minutes. Standing time: 3 minutes

Pungent garlic and fragrant lemon enhance the subtle flavor of rockfish in this simple but elegant entrée. Serve with rice or noodles to soak up the flavorful juices. (To prevent a watery sauce, always pat fish pieces dry before cooking.)

> 2 **tablespoons slivered almonds**
> ¼ **cup butter or margarine**
> 3 **cloves garlic, minced or pressed**
> 1 **tablespoon** *each* **lemon juice and chopped parsley**
> ¼ **teaspoon** *each* **paprika and grated lemon peel**
> ¾ **to 1 pound red snapper or lingcod fillets,** *each* **about ½ inch thick**
> **Lemon wedges**

Spread almonds on a rimmed microwave-proof plate. Microwave, uncovered, on **HIGH (100%)** for 6 to 8 minutes or until nuts are golden, stirring every 3 minutes. Set aside. (Almonds are soft after microwaving, but will firm up upon standing.)

Place butter, garlic, lemon juice, parsley, paprika, and lemon peel in a small microwave-proof bowl. Microwave, uncovered, on **HIGH (100%)** for 2 minutes or until heated through.

Pat fish dry and cut in serving-size pieces; then place in a 7 by 11-inch microwave-proof dish, with thickest portions toward outside of dish.

Pour butter mixture over fish and turn to coat all sides. Microwave, uncovered, on **HIGH (100%)** for 5

minutes; rotate each piece ½ turn after 3 minutes. Let stand for 3 minutes. Fish should flake readily when prodded in thickest portion with a fork. Arrange fish on a platter and pour juices over top; sprinkle with almonds. Serve lemon wedges alongside.

Sole and Chard with Hollandaise

 Preparation time: 17 minutes. Microwaving time: 12 minutes. Standing time: 3 minutes

Here's an elegant three-layer entrée: delicate sole fillets on a bed of shredded Swiss chard, with velvety hollandaise sauce spooned over all. Begin by steaming the chard; then arrange the sole atop, microwave briefly, and let stand until done. While the fish stands (and finishes cooking), prepare the egg-rich hollandaise. *NOTE:* Don't substitute spinach for chard—it doesn't hold up well in the microwave, and releases much more liquid than chard.

> 1 **pound Swiss chard, rinsed well and patted dry**
> 1 **pound sole fillets,** *each* **about ¼ inch thick, cut in serving-size pieces**
> 2 **tablespoons finely minced shallots**
> **Hollandaise sauce (recipe follows)**

Cut white stems of chard crosswise in ¼-inch slices and spread out on a microwave-proof platter. Cut leaves crosswise in thin strips; set aside. Cover platter with heavy-duty plastic wrap and microwave on **HIGH (100%)** for 2 minutes. Add leaves in a mound atop stems, re-cover, and microwave on **HIGH (100%)** for 2 minutes.

Pat fish dry; then place in a single layer atop steamed leaves, with thickest portions toward outside of platter. Spread shallots evenly over fish. Cover with heavy-duty plastic wrap and microwave on **HIGH (100%)** for 5 minutes, rotating each piece ½ turn after 3 minutes. Let stand for 3 minutes; fish should flake readily when prodded in thickest portion with a fork.

While fish stands, prepare hollandaise sauce. Drain and discard excess liquid from platter. Spoon a few tablespoons of hollandaise sauce over each piece of fish; pass remaining sauce at the table.

Hollandaise sauce. Place ½ cup (¼ lb.) **butter** or margarine in a 2-cup glass measure; microwave, uncovered, on **HIGH (100%)** for 1 minute or until melted. With a wire whisk, beat in 3 **egg yolks,** ½ cup **half-and-half** (light cream), ¼ teaspoon **dry mustard,** and 2 teaspoons **lemon juice.** Microwave, uncovered, on **HIGH (100%)** for 2 minutes or until sauce is slightly thickened; stir after 1 minute, then at 30-second intervals. (If sauce curdles, throw it out and start over.) Makes about ½ cup.

Egg and Ham Scramble

 Preparation time: 10 minutes. Microwaving time: 4 minutes. Standing time: 1 minute

Fluffy scrambled eggs dotted with ham and cheese make quick breakfast, brunch, or supper fare. To prevent eggs from overcooking, remove them from the oven while they're still moist—they'll continue to cook upon standing. (If they're moister than you like after standing, microwave them for 15 to 30 more seconds.) Serve with sliced tomatoes.

> 1 **tablespoon butter or margarine**
> 4 **eggs**
> ½ **cup milk**
> ⅛ **teaspoon salt**
>   **Dash of pepper**
> ¼ **cup finely minced cooked ham**
> ½ **cup shredded Cheddar cheese**

Place butter in a shallow 1-quart microwave-proof dish. Microwave, uncovered, on **HIGH (100%)** for 30 seconds or until melted. Break eggs into dish; add milk, salt, and pepper and beat with a wire whisk until well blended.

Microwave, uncovered, on **HIGH (100%)** for 1 minute. Stir in ham and ¼ cup of the cheese. Microwave, uncovered, on **HIGH (100%)** for 2 minutes; then stir, bringing cooked portion to inside of dish. Sprinkle with remaining ¼ cup cheese and microwave on **HIGH (100%)** for 30 more seconds. Let stand for 1 minute.

Eggs Benedict

 Preparation time: 15 minutes. Microwaving time: 6 minutes. Standing time: 2 to 4 minutes

The microwave is a natural for cooking up velvety sauces and poaching eggs in minutes. For perfect poached eggs, bring the water in the cups to a full boil, with bubbles breaking the surface, before you add the eggs. And *always remember to prick the membrane covering each yolk*—if you don't, you'll have egg spattered all over your oven.

> 4 **slices Canadian bacon or cooked ham, sliced ⅛ to ¼ inch thick**
> 2 **English muffins, split**
>   **Butter or margarine**
>   **Hollandaise sauce (page 91)**
> 4 **poached eggs (directions follow)**

In a wide frying pan over medium heat, cook bacon until lightly browned on both sides (about 1 minute per side). Meanwhile, toast muffin halves and spread with butter. Prepare hollandaise sauce; cover and keep warm while poaching eggs.

To serve, place 2 muffin halves on each of 2 plates. Cover each muffin half with a slice of bacon. Arrange one drained poached egg on each bacon-topped muffin; spoon hollandaise over each egg.

Poached eggs. Arrange four 10-ounce microwave-proof custard cups in a circle on a flat microwave-proof plate (this makes it easy to remove eggs all at once from oven). Pour ¼ cup **water** and ¼ teaspoon **white (distilled) vinegar** into each cup. Microwave, uncovered, on **HIGH (100%)** for 1 minute or until boiling.

Carefully break 1 **egg** into each cup. With a fork, prick through membrane covering each egg yolk; then cover each cup with heavy-duty plastic wrap. Microwave on **HIGH (100%)** for 2 minutes. Remove from oven and let stand for 2 minutes. (If you prefer your eggs firmer, let them stand for 3 to 4 minutes; they'll continue to cook in the hot water.) When eggs are done to your liking, immediately remove from water and drain briefly on paper towels.

Cheesy Potato Ramekins

 Preparation time: 20 minutes. Microwaving time: 12 minutes. Standing time: 3 minutes

Make tonight's dinner a vegetarian delight—with a casserole of cubed potatoes and sliced mushrooms in a creamy Swiss cheese sauce. Another time, try the casserole for brunch or lunch, perhaps accompanied with fresh fruit or a green salad.

The cheese in this recipe provides plenty of protein, but if you'd like a heartier dish (and you're not a vegetarian), you can add cubed ham.

> **Butter or margarine**
> 2 **medium-size thin-skinned potatoes (about 1 lb. total), peeled and cubed**
> ¼ **cup minced green onions, including some tops**
> ¼ **cup minced green pepper**
> ½ **cup whipping cream or half-and-half (light cream)**
> ¼ **pound small mushrooms, thinly sliced**
> 1 **cup cubed cooked ham (optional)**
> 1½ **cups (6 oz.) shredded Swiss cheese**
>   **Salt**

Generously butter two 5-inch microwave-proof ramekins. Evenly divide potatoes, onions, and green pepper between ramekins. Dot vegetables in each ramekin with 1 tablespoon butter, then pour ¼ cup cream into each. Cover loosely with heavy-duty plastic wrap. Microwave on **HIGH (100%)** for 8 minutes. Carefully remove plastic wrap, lifting it away from you to prevent steam from burning your hands.

Stir half the mushrooms into each ramekin. Microwave, uncovered, on **HIGH (100%)** for 3 minutes. Add ½ cup ham to each ramekin, if desired; then evenly sprinkle each with half the cheese and stir to combine. Microwave, uncovered, on **MEDIUM (50%)** for 1 minute. Cover and let stand for 3 minutes. Season to taste with salt.

Melted Cheese with Peppers

🕐 *Preparation time: 17 minutes. Microwaving time: 6 minutes. Standing time: None required—serve immediately (cheese solidifies upon standing)*

Around Guadalajara, Mexico, this simple appetizer is known as *queso fundido* ("melted cheese"). Our version, lightly seasoned with oregano, is hearty enough for a lunch or light supper entrée. You spread the cheese mixture on tortillas, top with a tomato salsa, roll up, and eat out of hand (provide plates to catch drips).

      Fresh tomato salsa (recipe follows)
2 **cups (8 oz.) shredded Mexican Chihuahua cheese, farmers cheese, or jack cheese**
¼ **teaspoon oregano leaves**
10 **thin strips** *each* **green pepper and onion**
6 **whole wheat or corn tortillas, warmed**

Prepare salsa and set aside. Toss together cheese and oregano; set aside. Place green pepper and onion on a 7-inch rimmed microwave-proof plate. Cover with heavy-duty plastic wrap and microwave on **HIGH (100%)** for 2 minutes or until vegetables are soft. Sprinkle cheese mixture over vegetables. Microwave, uncovered, on **MEDIUM (50%)** for 4 minutes or just until cheese is melted. Serve immediately.

To assemble, spread cheese mixture on a tortilla, spoon on a few tablespoons of salsa, roll up, and eat out of hand.

Fresh tomato salsa. In a bowl, combine 1 **tomato** (seeded and chopped), 2 tablespoons chopped **onion,** and 3 tablespoons *each* chopped **fresh cilantro** (coriander) and **canned diced California green chiles** (drained well).

Chile Egg Puff

🕐 *Preparation time: 10 minutes. Microwaving time: 13 minutes. Standing time: 10 minutes*

Unlike a soufflé, this south-of-the-border egg dish won't collapse when it's removed from the oven—it's stabilized with flour and an extra-large helping of cheese. After microwaving the puff, be sure to let it stand for ten full minutes; it takes this long for the eggs to set. Accompany with melon wedges and warmed tortillas; offer hot tomato-herb sauce to spoon on each portion (microwave the sauce just before serving).

4 **eggs**
2 **tablespoons all-purpose flour**
¼ **teaspoon baking powder**
    Dash of salt
1 **cup (4 oz.) shredded jack cheese**
2 **tablespoons butter or margarine, melted and slightly cooled**
2 **tablespoons canned diced California green chiles, drained well**
½ **cup small curd cottage cheese**
2 **tablespoons shredded Cheddar cheese**
    Tomato-herb sauce (recipe follows)

In a medium-size bowl, beat eggs until light and lemon-colored; then beat in flour, baking powder, salt, jack cheese, butter, chiles, and cottage cheese until well blended. Pour egg mixture into a 1-quart round microwave-proof dish. Cover with wax paper and microwave on **MEDIUM (50%)** for 10 minutes, rotating dish ½ turn after 5 minutes. Uncover and microwave on **HIGH (100%)** for 1 minute or just until center jiggles slightly when dish is gently shaken.

Sprinkle with Cheddar cheese; cover with wax paper and let stand for 10 minutes.

Just before serving, prepare tomato-herb sauce. Spoon egg puff onto individual plates and top each portion with some of the sauce.

Tomato-herb sauce. In a 2-cup glass measure, stir together 1 can (8 oz.) **tomato sauce,** 1 teaspoon chopped **chives,** and ¼ teaspoon *each* **ground cumin** and **oregano leaves.** Microwave, uncovered, on **HIGH (100%)** for 2 minutes (stirring after 1 minute) or until heated through.

Italian Tomato Fondue

🕐 Preparation time: 20 minutes. Microwaving time: 9 minutes. Standing time: None required—serve immediately (cheese solidifies upon standing)

Here's an Italian-style variation on Switzerland's famous hot cheese dip, ideal for a quick, light supper in summer or winter. It's served with slices of sausage, bread, and lots of vegetables, so you need add only a full-bodied red wine to complete the meal.

> **Assorted dippers: Carrot sticks, celery sticks, green pepper strips, zucchini rounds, cauliflowerets, Italian sausage slices, and bread sticks or cubes of firm Italian bread**

- 2 **cups (8 oz.) shredded Longhorn Cheddar cheese**
- ¼ **cup freshly grated Parmesan cheese**
- 2 **teaspoons cornstarch**
- 2 **tablespoons butter or margarine**
- 1 **small onion, finely minced**
- 1 **clove garlic, minced or pressed**
- 1 **can (8 oz.) stewed tomatoes, drained well**
- ½ **teaspoon dry basil**
- ⅛ **teaspoon pepper**

Prepare dippers; set aside. Toss together cheeses and cornstarch; set aside.

Place butter in a round 2-quart microwave-proof casserole or fondue dish. Microwave, uncovered, on **HIGH (100%)** for 30 seconds or until melted. Stir in onion and garlic; microwave, uncovered, on **HIGH (100%)** for 4 minutes or until vegetables are soft. Stir in tomatoes (break up with a spoon), basil, and pepper; cover with wax paper and microwave on **HIGH (100%)** for 2 minutes or until steaming.

Stirring constantly with a wooden spoon, gradually add cheese mixture, a few tablespoons at a time, stirring after each addition until cheese is melted. Then microwave, uncovered, on **MEDIUM (50%)** for 2 minutes or until fondue is thick and bubbly. Serve immediately, with assorted dippers.

To reheat, cover with wax paper and microwave on **MEDIUM (50%)** for 1 minute or until heated through.

How to Clean Leeks

Trim and discard root ends and all but 2 inches of dark green tops from leeks. Cut leeks in half lengthwise; rinse well under cold running water, separating layers to wash out all dirt. Place, cut side down, on paper towels; let drain thoroughly.

Beer and Cheddar Soup

🕐 Preparation time: 15 minutes. Microwaving time: 16 minutes. Standing time: 2 minutes

Rich, velvety, and laden with vegetables, these two cheese soups are sure to become popular choices for quick, hearty meals. Cheddar and beer flavor the first version; the second is a slightly thicker soup made with cream and Edam cheese (it's a favorite in the Netherlands). Serve either soup with bread sticks and a vinaigrette-dressed green salad.

A few tips for preparation: To ensure that the vegetables cook evenly, cut them all the same size (carrot pieces take a bit longer to cook than celery and leeks). Shred the cheese as finely as possible—the finer the shreds, the more quickly and evenly they'll melt. To prevent cheese from overheating (and thus turning stringy and tough), add it to the hot broth just a few tablespoons at a time, stirring until melted after each addition.

- 3 **tablespoons butter or margarine**
- 1 **cup e*ach* finely chopped carrots and celery**
- 1 **cup thinly sliced leeks**
- ¼ **teaspoon thyme leaves**
- 3 **tablespoons all-purpose flour**
- ¼ **teaspoon dry mustard**
- 1 **can (14½ oz.) regular-strength chicken broth**
- ½ **cup beer, at room temperature**
- 1 **cup (4 oz.) shredded sharp Cheddar cheese**

Place butter in a 1½-quart microwave-proof bowl. Microwave, uncovered, on **HIGH (100%)** for 45 seconds or until melted. Stir in carrots, celery, leeks, and thyme. Cover with wax paper and microwave on **HIGH (100%)** for 6 minutes (stirring after 3 minutes) or just until carrots are tender when pierced. Stir in flour and mustard. Microwave, uncovered, on **HIGH (100%)** for 1 minute.

Stirring constantly with a wooden spoon, gradually add broth; blend well. Cover with wax paper and microwave on **HIGH (100%)** for 6 minutes (stirring after 3 minutes) or until broth is thickened. Stir in beer, re-cover, and microwave on **HIGH (100%)** for 2 minutes. Stir in cheese, a few tablespoons at a time, stirring after each addition until cheese is melted. Let stand for 2 minutes.

Leek and Edam Soup

Follow directions for **Beer and Cheddar Soup,** but omit carrots and celery and use 3 cups thinly sliced leeks. Omit thyme and mustard; instead, use ¼ teaspoon *each* **pepper** and **ground mace.** Substitute 1 can (14½ oz.) **regular-strength beef broth** for chicken broth, ½ cup **whipping cream** for beer, and 1 cup (4 oz.) shredded **Edam or Gouda cheese** for Cheddar.

Index

Metric Conversion Table

To change	To	Multiply by
ounces (oz.)	grams (g)	28
pounds (lb.)	kilograms (kg)	0.45
teaspoons	milliliters (ml)	5
tablespoons	milliliters (ml)	15
fluid ounces (oz.)	milliliters (ml)	30
cups	liters (l)	0.24
pints (pt.)	liters (l)	0.47
quarts (qt.)	liters (l)	0.95
gallons (gal.)	liters (l)	3.8
Fahrenheit temperature (°F)	Celsius temperature (°C)	5/9 after subtracting 32